Stories
& Object Lessons

Children's
Stories
& Object Lessons

A Sourcebook
for Christian
Storytellers

Marvin
Hunt

REVIEW AND HERALD® PUBLISHING ASSOCIATION
HAGERSTOWN, MD 21740

The author assumes full responsibility for the accuracy of all facts and quotations as cited in this book.

Texts credited to NEB are from *The New English Bible*. © The Delegates of the Oxford University Press and the Syndics of the Cambridge University Press 1961, 1970. Reprinted by permission.

Texts credited to NIV are from the *Holy Bible, New International Version*. Copyright © 1973, 1978, 1984, International Bible Society. Used by permission of Zondervan Bible Publishers.

Bible texts credited to TEV are from the *Good News Bible*—Old Testament: Copyright © American Bible Society 1976; New Testament: Copyright © American Bible Society 1966, 1971, 1976.

This book was
Edited by Richard W. Coffen
Designed by Patricia S. Wegh
Cover design by Bryan Gray
Cover photos by Joel D. Springer
Typeset: 11.5/13.5 Times

PRINTED IN U.S.A.

99 98 97 96 95   5 4 3 2 1

R&H Cataloging Service
Hunt, Marvin
    Children's stories & object lessons: a sourcebook for Christian storytellers.

    1. Storytelling.   2. Storytelling—Collections.   I Title.

372.64202

ISBN 0-8280-0948-1

Dedication

This book is dedicated
to the memory of
Traudl Heidi Hunt
(1942-1992)

Acknowledgments

As a young minister I had the privilege to receive training from a master storyteller and returned African missionary, Foster Medford. I owe very much to Grand Medford. Also, I was given the opportunity to observe and learn from the acclaimed author and storyteller, Dr. James Tucker. Later on at the university, Professor Bill Emerson taught me to "turn my telescope around and take a closer look at life." And finally a special thank you to my friend, Jennifer Rash, the English teacher who has long encouraged me in the art of crafting vignettes and writing. To rephrase Alfred Lord Tennyson, "All whom I have met, have become a little part of me."

Special Appreciation

The following people allowed me to retell their stories with the hope that their experiences could benefit and encourage others:

Jerry Abernathy	Tom Hunt
The Baker Family	Gerald Linderman
Joe Blevins	Seaborn Martin
Vita Bresee	Mom
D. J. Cain	Trudel (Kovarsch) Moore
Wayne Cagle	Jason Parker
Homer Deal	Georg Saliba
Myron Eberhardt	Morris Venden
Judy Crowe Hunt	Dortch Williams

Do you have a story that should be told time and time again? Please send it to:

MARVIN HUNT
c/o REVIEW AND HERALD® PUBLISHING ASSOCIATION
55 WEST OAK RIDGE DRIVE
HAGERSTOWN, MD 21740

There are no guarantees, but we would like to consider your story.

Contents

PART III   OBJECT LESSONS

Before you read this book . . .

This book is intended for use by ministers, teachers, and laypersons—anyone who speaks to children assembled in groups. The purpose is to aid leaders in using persuasion to help young people develop strong Christian characters. This art is a powerful tool and can be very effective in making long—term changes in young people's lives.

As Erwin Bettinghaus says in his book *Persuasive Communication*: "Animals tend to solve their disputes by fighting or by pretending to fight. Dogs growl, cats hiss, lions roar, and elephants trumpet their displeasure when another member of the species trespasses on their territory. When growling, hissing, roaring, and trumpeting fail to work, fighting tends to occur. The winner takes the territory, or the female, or the bone. The side of the mighty becomes equated with the side of the right.

"Mankind also resorts to fighting, and a look at world history will show relatively few years in which bitter struggles involving thousands of men were not occurring. A pessimistic look at the history of man might lead one to conclude that he is no better off than any other animal or even that he is worse off because he wages war more effectively than any animal.

"There is a more optimistic view. In the largest percentage of all human interaction situations the basic decision-making tool is not fighting, not biting, not roaring, not hissing, but persuading. Over the centuries, man has come to depend more and more on persuasion as the basic tool for accomplishing change" (p. 1).

As Christian storytellers our goal is to persuade children to accept Jesus Christ as their personal Saviour. That means persuading them to surrender their hearts and change their minds.

Concerning change, an illustration called the "hub model of beliefs, attitudes, and values" might help illustrate what persuasion hopes to accomplish. Imagine drawing a large circle on a sheet of notebook paper, and then within that circle drawing another circle about half size, and then finally a tiny circle in the center. The drawing would look something like a target with a bull's-eye center. Now imagine labeling the outer circle as "beliefs," the middle circle as "attitudes," and the inner bull's-eye as "values." This drawing suggests how the human mind works. The outer circle, beliefs, is the easiest to change. The middle circle, attitudes, is harder to modify, and finally, the inner core of our values is the most difficult to alter. As persuaders we attempt story by story to work our way through the layers and get to the very core of young people so as to affect their values.

To help readers be better persuaders, this book contains stories, illustrations, and object lessons that are based on real-life experiences that are as true to detail as the author can determine. The illustrations and object lessons are drawn from everyday life situations to which children and adults alike can easily relate.

To reiterate: the purpose of this book is to help *you* persuade young people to develop strong Christian characters, which come from a personal relationship with Christ. Character-building stories have their place, but for Christians, stories without Jesus Christ at the center are off the mark.

PART I

INTRODUCTION

Chapter 1

Advice for Beginning Storytellers

So you want to tell a children's story but you don't know where to start? Well, why not accept that there are few born storytellers. Most of us must learn the hard way. We master the art of telling stories just as we learned a subject in school. We commit to memory the basics, and then we move on to do what we have learned. Perfection comes with practice, or as the old maxim states: "Practice makes perfect."

I vividly remember the first time I stood before a group of children in a little church in Ohio and trembled with fear while reading a story verbatim from a book. The children, the congregation, and I were all greatly relieved when the story was finished! However, it was the beginning of an experience that has been rewarding and gratifying. As an outgrowth of my experiences, the following is a series of steps gleaned from many sources that can help you develop into a first-class storyteller yourself.

What Is a Story?

Many people think of a story simply as something written down in a book to be read to children again and again. Few have thought through what goes into making a children's story because they have had no reason to analyze one. It's like driving a car—you learn a few rudimentary things about how to operate the brakes and the gas, then you memorize some traffic rules, and after taking a test, you're given a license. However, if you decide you want to be a race car driver in the Indianapolis 500, things change drastically. It doesn't take long to realize that an automobile is a very complex machine that reacts to aerodynamic forces and all sorts of physical laws of which you never dreamed. So too is the relative degree of complexity in what makes the difference between a story reader and a storyteller. Would-be storytellers, welcome to the fast lane!

Let's begin by defining what a story is.

A story is a picture painted with words that has one specific purpose. It is basically a patchwork quilt of words sewn together with the threads of the life experiences of the storyteller. Many effective stories often begin with the words "When I was about your age I . . ." Stories are your opportunities to cause young people to think differently. Well-crafted stories seek to influence children to make life-changing decisions. They are not just entertainment. Rather, stories are teaching vehicles that are used to inspire children to develop the qualities of character that will motivate them to be solid Christian young people and honorable citizens for the rest of their lives.

Objectives and Philosophy

To begin, you must have a definite goal. Don't be like the proverbial rider who got on his horse and rode off in all directions. You will want to follow three steps in organizing a story: (1) determine the subject, (2) select a theme, and (3) make a proposition to build your story around.

For example, kids who disapprove of self-control is a good subject, but a theme of self-control at school adds emphasis. An even more clearly defined theme would be self-control at school when someone wants to give you some free drugs. The proposition derived might be: *"By the grace of God, Christian boys and girls can overcome Satan's temptations and realize that every mousetrap has free cheese"* (see object lesson 8).

Good stories are like rifle shots, straight and to the point. Stories without a point are like shotgun blasts in which one shoots with the hope of hitting something . . . anything! Before all else, formulate a definite theme for the story you are going to tell. Develop the KISS principle—

Keep
It
Simple and
Sweet!

Realize that children are human beings in development. They may lack the years of experience that adults take for granted, but they are still pliable, teachable possibilities. Many adults expect children to act as if they were 30 years old and deeply interested in the story being told. However, children do not have the inhibitions of trying to be socially correct or polite. If they are bored, they let you know it. If they are interested, they also make you aware of it. "If children are little rats to you, they will run. . . . But if, apart from faults and apart from virtues, you take them as something very precious to love, they will be yours forever" (Arthur W. Spalding and Eric B. Hare, *Christian Storytelling*, p. 10).

Even though they may squirm a lot, seem inattentive, or give you "dumb" answers when you ask a question, never embarrass them. All children are worthy of being taught. Understand that children under the age of 7 or 8 are not able to grasp abstractions. A typical conversation might run:

Child: "Am I 5?"

Parent: "Yes, you're 5 years old."

Child: "What's a years?"

Parent: "A year is a lot of days all added together. It takes 365 days to make a year."

Child: "Is that a long time?"

Parent: "Yes, dear, that's a long time."

Children learn in a process that leads them from objects they can touch and feel to more abstract things. For instance, a child will understand the word "dog" to refer to the family pet. But as the child develops, he or she learns to group many single individuals into the category of dog. Eventually the child understands that dogs belong in an even larger group called animals. As the process of learning progresses, the child is able to understand the higher abstract concepts such as right, wrong, beauty, and truth.

Know Your Competition

Realize what you are up against! Most children today spend endless hours in front of the television or playing video games. Phil

Phillips, in his book *Saturday Morning Mind Control*, describes the challenge this way: "Young Child sits in front of The Box as a student sits in front of a teacher.

"Today's lesson is violence. The Box will teach you how to punch, kick, and fight and that aggression is the prime means of resolving conflict. Never mind, Young Child, that the world operates differently.

"Tomorrow's lesson involves social studies. The Box will present the world as it is perceived by television producers-to-be. Be aware, Young Child, that what you learn won't translate into real life.

"The Box will also include lessons about sexuality and about drugs. We hope, Young Child, that you will ignore these messages. Nevertheless, they are part of the curriculum.

"The Box will teach you how to shop, what to choose, and what is in. At least, Young Child, The Box will teach you what it has been paid to teach you, and along the way, you'll get an education in consumerism and materialism.

"Finally, The Box will teach you religion. It probably won't teach you the religion that your parents are trying to teach you, Young Child, but never mind. You'll get hours of instruction free of charge, and that will more than offset the few minutes of Sunday school, church, synagogue, or other catechism that your parents offer. You'll be adept at recognizing and manipulating occult symbols and techniques, and Eastern religions will seem like second nature to you.

"All of the education with free tuition is from The Box.

"Get ready, Young Child. School is in session!" (p. 47).

Today the storyteller's effectiveness is lost after five to seven minutes mainly because of shortened attention spans, which in turn may result from watching too many videos. "The average person will see some 30,000 electronic stories before he or she reaches the age of twenty-one" (*ibid.*, p. 20). However, this is not a reason to give up and simply copy the competition. Instead, it is an opportunity to show the children better alternatives.

One should also remember that the things we take for granted as part of everyday life are new and different to children's young minds. Their world is seen from the perspective of just being tall enough to look over the kitchen counter, or maybe being able to finally see out a car window . . . from the back seat!

Whenever possible, reference your stories to Scripture. Jesus' life and the Psalms and the Proverbs in God's Word are rich with pithy statements around which to center your story. However, finding just the right scriptural reference is not always easy or necessary. If you reach an impasse, a reminder for the children to be like Jesus will underscore your point nicely. After all, the exemplary life of Jesus is the example all Christians seek to follow.

Take the time to consider whether your story is positive or negative. Certainly there are hard lessons to be learned from disobedience, but there are also positive ways of presenting the same lessons. If your stories tell only of punishment, injuries, and mishaps, they soon become dry lectures that the children will dread. Indeed, there is a place for somber, reality-based stories, but they must be liberally surrounded by positive, upbeat messages. The stories in this book alternate between positive and negative for a more balanced presentation.

Sadly, one must consider the effects of divorce on children. In a survey of Americans by Rubenstein and Shaver (1982), cited in the book *Social Psychology* (sixth edition), we read: "First, children often blame themselves for the divorce. . . . The legacy of this self-blame can be persistent low self-esteem—an enduring belief that one is unlovable and unworthy of affection. . . . Rubenstein and Shaver also speculate that children of divorce may come to see other people as rejecting and unreliable" (p. 235).

Considering the many serious effects of divorce or the loss of a parent through death or being born out of wedlock, a storyteller should always be careful about using the terms referring to parents. As one elementary school teacher noted, "I asked my kids to write about what they would do if they were president of the United States. One of them wrote that he would see that every boy and girl had a mommy and a daddy."

Methods

If you are telling someone else's story, read it aloud to yourself and share it only if you yourself can enjoy and appreciate it. Modify the story to fit your personality. Successful storytellers come in many varieties. One person may be comfortable crawling around on the floor and barking like a dog, whereas another finds the idea completely repulsive. There is no black and white method that works for everyone. Instead, the adage of working in one's own harness is more appropriate.

Speak to the children, not the adults. Use a child's vocabulary when possible. If you must use a big word, explain the meaning if it is not too involved. Visualize how the characters look, the clothing they wear, and how they act. Imagine the action of the story as if it is seen in a series of pictures. Try to see, live, and feel your story— as a child might. Don't lose your child's point of view. Love as a child. Understand as a child. Have a sense of humor, and use it to relax your hearers.

The book *Principles of Speech Communication* by Monroe and Ehninger (sixth brief edition), lists five types of ineffective speakers (p. 7):

Elocutionists—those who talk to display personal skills rather than to communicate ideas. Such people permit themselves to be carried away by the sound of their voice and the graceful manipulation of their body, and forget that their purpose is to induce other people to understand, enjoy, or believe what they are saying.

Verbal Gymnasts—those who make a parade of language. They never use a familiar word if they can find an esoteric one. They delight in complex sentences and mouth-filling phrases. Disraeli once described the verbal gymnast as a man "intoxicated with the exuberance of his own verbosity."

Gibberers—those who emit a continuous stream of words with little or no thought behind them. They jump from one point to another until the listeners are thoroughly confused. They usually conclude their speech with the abrupt remark "Well, I guess that's all I have to say on the subject."

Hermits—those who mumble to themselves. They may have a wealth of ideas that are well-organized and developed, but they direct them to the ceiling or floor, talk in a weak or monotonous voice, and make no effort to be heard or understood.

Culprits—Those who seem to be ashamed of what they are saying. They shrink from the hearers both in voice and manner. Sometimes they apologize verbally and always seem to be self-conscious and tentative. Instead of being firm and forthright in their statements, they give the impression that they do not believe themselves.

To be a more effective speaker, stand where the children can see you and speak so that they can hear you. Whenever possible, use props or visual aids. "Make it clear—use the eye as well as the ear." The more familiar the object you use, the more often they will be reminded of the lesson. "Every time you see the sun shining bright, think of Jesus, the light of the world."

There is a communication process that takes place as you tell your story. It is likened to a telephone conversation. There is the sender, the noise on the telephone line, the receiver of the message at the other end, and your reaction to how the receiver responds to you. What is finally understood by the hearer is the result of what you actually said and what the listener thought he or she heard. For instance, if there is "noise" on the phone line or for a storyteller—a youngster chattering or playing while you are talking—the distraction affects how your message is received. What you said or thought you said may not have been heard. If you see that glazed look in their eyes, double back and repeat your message after the noise has cleared from the line.

Another source of noise on the line can be your bearing or credibility with the children. It is easier for the children to agree with people they like. Because they like you, they will be more willing to change. There is also a second factor: children will be influenced more by people who are like them. Remind the children that you also had a childhood and that you know what it is like to be a child. "When I was just about your age, I remember getting into really big trouble when I . . ."

When you stand in front of the children, 40 percent of what they take in is from nonverbal communications or things we say without using words. This includes body language, clothes, makeup, hair styles, etc.

The use of your body to communicate is crucial. Establishing eye contact with the children is the first thing you should do. They should feel that you are talking to each of them personally. Your gestures should be natural and appropriate to the story you are telling. The six basic gestures of the hands include cautioning, clenching of your fist, rejecting, dividing, giving or receiving, and pointing. Practice them—along with gestures of the head, shoulders, and facial expressions—until they become a natural part of your presentation.

Use your face as a picture of your story. If the story is sad, look sad; conversely, if the story is happy, appear that way. This may sound obvious, but it does not always come easy to everyone. It may take some practice, but if we live our story, it will naturally reflect from our face, and the children will immediately respond. Many people use a mirror or a video camera as an aid in practicing all gestures. As in all the arts, it is through practice that we perfect our skills. A good place to start, if you have children at home, is by telling them your story.

Another aspect of nonverbal communication is what we wear. Clothing can have such a forceful impact that there was a time when powerful nobles passed laws forbidding peasants from wearing bright and colorful garments. Satins, silks, and furs were powerful nonverbal communicators. The drably dressed peasant knew his lowly place—his clothes told him so. The modern-day lesson is obvious.

Children of all ages always respond to plenty of action and presentations in which they can participate. They like hands-on things that they can touch and feel. This is especially true if you bring in live animals and pets. If you can put the animal (or any object lesson, for that matter) in a sack and rattle the bag a few times, you will always have the undivided attention of your children.

However, beware: animals often have a mind of their own. A lady brought her kitten in a box to Vacation Bible School. When she opened the carton, the frightened cat, which had been shut up in the dark, made a dash for freedom, scratching its owner and racing off into the woods. The children cried for the lost cat, the lady had a scratched hand, and the lesson was unsalvageable. Another example of a good idea gone sour was the college professor who brought a live snake to pass around. Some of the kids loved it, some ran for cover, and others just sat paralyzed with fear. He would have been more successful if he had presented it in a cage. Afterward he could have allowed the braver ones to handle the animal. Indeed, if you plan your presentations carefully, the world of nature is an inexhaustible storehouse of stories and object lessons to fascinate video-jaded young people.

Another thought on arresting children's attention: if you don't have a bag to rattle or an animal in a cage, begin by asking a question. For instance, "Have any of you ever seen a bird wearing a hat?" The answer is obvious, but the question has piqued their interest.

Telling stories or creating object lessons in which the children can directly participate is also important. Phil Phillips states: "Over the years, educators have concluded that persons commit to memory and put into action about 10 percent of what they hear, 50 percent of what they see, and 90 percent of what they do" *(Saturday Morning Mind Control*, p. 12).

Another type of presentation that works well for small groups in classroom settings is brainstorming. The presenter asks the children to make suggestions, which are then written on a blackboard. For example, one can divide the blackboard into two parts, positive and negative, and ask the students to suggest what the word "character" means. The presenter explains that there are bad character traits and good ones.

Under the heading "Positive Character Traits" the students can suggest all the positive things they like in other people. Then the process is repeated under the heading "Negative Character Traits." Once the list is complete, ask: "Who are the positive attributes similar to? Who are the negative attributes similar to?" Of course, all the good characteristics are like Jesus, and the conclusion is that we should be like Him. This type of presentation encourages all members of the group to participate and also permits them to draw their own conclusion concerning the topic. Brainstorming works best in a classroom setting and can include topics such as obedience, music, dress, telling the truth, etc. (see object lesson 15).

Finally, after you have done everything right, relate a convincing conclusion. Every story should have a definite beginning, middle, and end! Most fall short on the ending. A simple formula for storytelling is get their attention at the beginning, put the facts in the middle, and close with an emotional appeal. Do not moralize at the end. Instead, restate the theme, but don't get into an endless loop of repeating yourself. As the old axiom goes for preachers: "Stand up, speak up, and sum it up!"

Tips on Presentation

If your presentation is in church, assemble the children on the steps of the platform so that the adults can see their reactions. Remember that you are also speaking to the adults. Keep them in the back of your mind, but don't use the story as a vehicle to lecture the adults. It is appropriate, however, to turn to the church now and then to make a point or also to show the people the visual aid you may be using.

Beginners should seriously consider using an assistant to help tell the story. Novices who are nervous and unsure find it a comforting feeling to have someone standing nearby to prompt them if they forget a detail in the story. Writing out an outline on a small index card that you hold in the palm of your hand is always a good idea as are cue cards laid on the floor. Even if you don't use them, the security of knowing that they are there will help you be a better storyteller.

There is another reason for using an assistant. Often parents expect miracles of storytellers. It is not unusual for parents to bring the smallest of children to hear the story. They smile and set them down and leave them unattended in your care. Since most of your stories will be targeted at children ages 6 through 12, infants and toddlers are an impossible assignment. An assistant can be invaluable in seeing that your story gets heard by most of the children.

Murphy's law will likely get you. If you use visual aids or props, keep them as simple as possible, and be sure to test them beforehand. Children are unimpressed with the statement "Well, I thought this would work."

After the Story Is Told

Remember that children lack the handicap of politeness, and every storyteller fails sometimes. Get constructive criticism from a friend who will tell you the truth. Was your story too short, too long, boring? Did you use too many big words? Was your story beyond the experience of a child's world? Was the story good? If so, what made it good? Ask your critic, "If you could change the story, what would you change?" Most of all, learn from your experiences, but don't take your storytelling too seriously! If you erred or messed up on the story line, chances are the children never knew it. Keep on trying to develop your skills into what they should be—a vehicle that will enable you to laugh and have fun with a group of great young people, all the while teaching them principles that will affect their lives eternally.

Other Story Sources

Life is full of character-building stories. The problem is finding good stories and then being able to buff them up for the children to hear in such a way that they will never forget either the story or the point.

The first response of most people when they are asked if they know any good stories is "I had a boring childhood" or "I was a good child growing up; I never got into much trouble." My response is always the same—children's stories are about real children and their everyday lives. After all, few of us have been skydiving off the Empire State Building or were childhood alligator wrestlers. The best stories come from everyday life, using everyday examples just as Jesus did when He talked to the people. In His stories a sower went forth to sow, a fisherman cast his net, a lady swept her house as she looked for a lost coin, and some weeds grew up in the wheat field.

Storytellers learn to probe deeper and are usually rewarded with stories like "Well, there was the time when I was a little boy and picked up a pretty little fly in the kitchen window. I discovered that pretty little flies are called yellow jackets and that they really hurt when they sting! I know because it stung me when I tried to pick it up. I guess things aren't always what they seem." This little story is a natural. It contains enough elements around which to build a good lesson.

After finding a story with potential, go through the journalist's checklist and ask who? what? where? why? when? and how? For the sake of accuracy, be sure to write the information down. While good true stories may not abound, a person who is diligent can glean good ones here and there, and then polish them into treasures that the children will always remember.

Another good source for stories is the *Minister's Manual*, edited by James W. Cox and published by Harper Collins, New York. This book contains an excellent collection of weekly children's stories and sermons, and is available at Christian bookstores.

Also Christian bookstores and libraries are a standard source of stories and object lessons.

Some Important Concluding Thoughts

When I tell children stories, I keep a certain twinkle in my eye, compassion in my heart, and Jesus on my mind. It shows all over my face. In my opinion there is never an appropriate occasion to scare children into being good. The principle taught in the old adage that "only volunteers will go to heaven" also applies to Christian storytelling. Children can be told of experiences that are negative in a kind and compassionate manner. Then the children, once they understand the negative side, become responsible to make up their own minds, and as volunteers to do what is right. Children can tell by your demeanor when you are trying to love them into the safety of the fold. They know when you are talking from your heart and urging them to do right because it is for their own good.

Also, there is the constant need always to use a generous amount of an uncommon commodity called common sense. This is especially important when doing object lessons. I think of an example of how tragedy can strike in a totally unexpected way. The incident as I was told took place when a minister, who was standing in a baptistry full of water, reached up and touched a microphone. The mistake was fatal. May I underscore the lesson here: If you are using an electrical appliance, fire, chemicals, or anything that could remotely cause harm, think again. Take a second look to see if you can discover a safer way to make the same point.

And, finally, may God's blessing be upon you as you undertake the formidable task of being a Christian storyteller.

PART II

STORIES

Angels Watching Over Me
. . . and You

"He who walks with the wise grows wise, but a companion of fools suffers harm" (Prov. 13:20, NIV).

Gas Tank Hank and the neighbor kids used to walk home from school because they didn't want to ride the bus. They said it took too long to get home because of the route and many bus stops along the way. To take the shortest way home, Gas Tank Hank often cut through a golf course. In Ohio, where Hank grew up, it often gets very cold in the winter, so golf courses close because of the snow and ice. No one was around that day because the course was closed for the winter, and it wasn't unusual for Hank and his friends to play around the golf course equipment buildings as they made their way home.

However, they did know that they were trespassing. Gas Tank Hank knew that they were not supposed to be on the golf course grounds, but he and his friends would sneak in anyway. After all, they thought, who would ever find out?

One afternoon they cut through the woods behind the golf course and came out by a shed where lawn mowers and tractors were kept. Outside the shed sat a large gasoline tank with a hand pump and long hose to fill the equipment with fuel. It was always locked . . . except for this time. At first the boys were afraid and thought somebody might have broken the lock off to steal gas. But as the boys stood around and talked, someone wondered out loud if there was any gas left. One of them went over and began turning the pump handle round and round until out spit a gallon or two of gasoline onto the ground.

As the gas was pouring out, one of Hank's friends became afraid that they might be accused of breaking the lock, so he nervously tried to get everyone to leave. It was just as they were leaving that one of the boys—and it wasn't Hank this time wondered—what would happen if they struck a match. So one of them reached into his pocket and pulled out a pack of matches, and before anyone knew what happened, the gasoline on the ground exploded into flames. The ball of fire immediately singed everyone's eyebrows and hair. They all ran like crazy to get away from the fire. However, when they turned around, they realized that the flames were all over the grass surrounding the gas tank.

They knew that if the tank exploded, it would burn down the maintenance shed and all the buildings around it. The whole golf course would go up in flames. That's when they ran back and beat out the fire with their coats.

Praise God, the tank didn't explode! Surely their guardian angels were shaking their heads as they were watching the boys put out the fire.

You know, those boys were twice foolish. First, they didn't have any business playing around on the golf course or near its buildings. The golf course was private property, and they were breaking the law. Second, they stood by and let their friend light the match. All they had to say was no and take the matches away from him. It was as simple as . . . just say no! "No, I won't do that," or "No, I won't let you do that!"

The next time someone asks you to do something you know is wrong, remember the gasoline tank and how Gas Tank Hank got his name. Just say no to doing or to helping do something you know is wrong, and you'll always be doing what is right!

Burglar Alarms

When Fearless Frank was about your age, he was afraid of the dark. Noises in the night always scared him. He was always worrying that someone was hiding next door in his parents' room behind his mother's dresser. That was because the dresser sat across the corner of the room, and there was a big space behind it where Frank used to play hide-and-seek.

Fearless Frank was really a chicken. He imagined that a bank robber or some escaped prisoner could sneak into his house during the day when no one was home and hide out. I guess you could say he was a real scaredy-cat. He always got more worried when it was time to go to bed. At night he had to go upstairs to his room, and he just *knew* that a bad person would be waiting behind his mother's dresser to get him. To make matters worse, his house was always making creaking and popping sounds late at night when everyone else was fast asleep. It all seemed so scary!

Fearless Frank was so afraid that he finally decided to build a homemade burglar alarm and hook it onto his bedroom door for protection. One night he tied one end of a string to the door knob of his room. Then he ran the string up in the air, fastened some of his mother's glass dishes to the other end of the string, and hung the dishes over a pile of pots and pans. When the door was opened, the dishes would fall down and crash together, warning him that someone was trying to get into his room.

Well, it worked . . . kind of. It just so happened that the night he built the burglar alarm his father decided to check on him one more time before he went to bed. It must have been very late, and Frank was in a deep sleep. All he knew was that the dishes crashed, his father just about jumped out of his skin, and Fearless Frank sat bolt upright in bed! Fearless Frank had caught his own father with his alarm! Needless to say, Father made it clear that Frank didn't need

35

a burglar alarm anymore. He thought what Fearless Frank really needed was some courage.

That was many years ago. Today in Frank's house things still go bump in the night and wake him up. But he's learned that all houses make creaking and cracking sounds. Doesn't yours? It's because they heat up during the day, when the sun shines on the roof. The heat makes the wooden beams in the attic expand or move just a little bit, and when they do that they make funny noises. At night the same wooden parts cool back down, and the beams in the attic move again. This heating and cooling, expanding and shrinking, makes some houses crack and pop all night long. It's scary, but it's not dangerous.

And furthermore, because Frank is now a Christian, he finally has the courage he once lacked. Now he has the faith to believe that Jesus will protect him and his home. Noises still wake him up, but he can go back to sleep knowing that the Lord is his shepherd. He's your shepherd, too. Trust in Him, and He will give you sweet sleep.

"The Lord is my shepherd; I have everything I need. . . . Even if I go through the deepest darkness, I will not be afraid, Lord, for you are with me" (Ps. 23:1-4, TEV).

Arial and Cassie Pray for the Abandoned Birds

House wrens build their nests in the strangest places. It's not unusual for them to build in an old hat hanging on the garage wall, or even in an old shoe. This is a story about a wren that built her nest in a little toolbox just one foot from the back door of Cassie and Arial's house in the Georgia mountains.

Day after day the little wren sat patiently on her eggs as the people walked back and forth across the porch. She would sit dead still, hoping they wouldn't notice her as they passed her little nest on the way into their house. Arial and Cassie looked at her when they passed, but they never bothered the little mother. Finally, four tiny baby wrens hatched. As the days passed, the mother fed them lots of bugs and other things that wrens eat. The babies grew and developed fluffy little feathers. It's called fledging out.

Then something very bad happened. The family went to church one day, and when they came back home, the mother wren had disappeared. They waited and waited for her to show up, but she never came back. Something terrible must have happened to her. The baby birds began to starve. One day passed, and then two days, and still the mother didn't show up. Cassie and Arial's parents tried to find someone to tell them what to feed the hungry birds, but no one they asked knew what to do. No matter what they tried feeding them, they wouldn't eat. Everyone felt so helpless watching the little birds die. Finally, Mother and Father gave up and decided to take the nest out into the woods and let the birds die quietly. There was nothing anyone could do for the starving birds.

However, before they put the birds in the woods, Cassie and Arial asked if they could pray for the birds in their evening prayers. They prayed earnestly for God to help save the little birds. They went to bed in the faith that they would be happy with whatever God decided to do.

The next morning a miracle happened! The back porch looked like a busy airport, with birds flying everywhere. The birds were waiting in line to feed the chicks. It was wonderful! Birds that were not even related to wrens lined up to feed the babies. A bright yellow-and-black goldfinch seemed to be the leader. Arial and Cassie's dad said when he went onto the porch that he was even fusscd at by the birds waiting their turn to feed the chicks! Cassie and Arial's mom and dad checked the nest every night and found no adult bird staying with the babies. They stayed alone every night and kept warm by squeezing up to one another. However, during the day their foster parents fed them faithfully. The birds continued to feed them for two more weeks until the baby wrens finally got all their feathers and flew off on their own.

Jesus said: *"Do not be afraid; you are worth much more than many sparrows!" (Matt. 10:31, TEV).* Arial and Cassie will tell you that Jesus answers prayers, and they know that if Jesus will care for four starving house wrens, He will also care for you!

It's Always Better to Stick Together

"How wonderful it is, how pleasant, for God's people to live together in harmony!" (Ps. 133:1, TEV).

Birds eat all kinds of things. Some birds even eat bees and wasps. They leap off their perch and snatch these stinging insects right out of the air as they fly by. The European bee-eater, a bird that actually comes from Africa, hitchhikes a ride when he can't find a tree to perch in. He sits on the backs of ostriches and sheep, and rides along looking for bees and wasps to catch. Here in America we have two types of bee-eating birds, but they don't ride on animals' backs. The more common name for them is the eastern kingbird and the summer tanager. Both birds also eat other things. The kingbird eats some 400 different types of insects, and the summer tanager also likes grubs.

However, a little lady in Georgia named Ms. Vida discovered that there is another kind of bird that will also eat insects that sting. It's the eastern bluebird, which normally eats crawling insects. Most often bluebirds are seen fluttering to the ground to catch beetles, crickets, grasshoppers, or an occasional lizard or tree frog.

However, Ms. Vida found out that bluebirds will also eat wasps if they have to. She made her discovery one day when she was planting lilies in her garden. After setting the plants in the flower bed, she went to get the garden hose to water them. While uncoiling the hose from its rack, she stirred up some yellow jackets, which are known for their very bad tempers. They had built their nest under the hose rack, where she couldn't see them.

Before she could get away, one of them stung her on the lip. Then the rest of them, still upset and angry, flew off after some bluebirds that were nesting nearby. Ms. Vida said she turned around and looked up to see the yellow jackets chasing the birds way up high in the sky. She said she was surprised to see that the little wasps were getting the better of the bluebirds as they circled around overhead.

But the story does not end with a victory for the yellow jackets. Things took an amazing turn when Ms. Vida went back to working with her lilies. Eventually the yellow jackets settled down and went back into their nest to go about their normal duties. Suddenly a bluebird showed up and perched just outside the yellow jackets' nest. It waited. Ms. Vida couldn't believe her eyes when she saw what happened next. Each time a yellow jacket would leave the nest, the bird would catch it and gobble it up! One by one the bluebird snatched the wasps out of the air and ate every one! It ate so many yellow jackets that Ms. Vida thought it would pop.

The bird won the battle one yellow jacket at a time. In this case, the yellow jackets lost because of two reasons. They should have left the bluebirds alone—after all, the birds were minding their own business before they were attacked. The next mistake the yellow jackets made was that they forgot to stick together. After everything seemed quiet and peaceful, they let down their guard.

So it is with you and me. The devil knows that if he can get us off by ourselves where we don't belong, we're in big trouble! We need to stay in our own yard. We need to know where we can and cannot go, and then stay where we belong. Second, Christians must stick together, families must stick together, and friends must stick together. Another word for sticking together is unity. The Bible says: *"How good and pleasant it is when brothers [people] live together in unity" (Ps. 133:1, NIV).*

Birds With Suitcases

Have you ever helped pack to go on vacation? Do you remember all those suitcases full of clothes and shoes? If you went to the beach, you probably packed a radio, chairs, an umbrella, plus beach towels, a hat, and all kinds of other things people carry along on vacation. Sometimes it won't all fit in the car, so people carry the extra stuff on top of their car. Perhaps you've seen cars with a thing strapped to the top that looks like a big hamburger box from McDonald's. Of course, you know that it's full of all the stuff they couldn't fit inside the car. Sometimes you even see bicycles and tricycles tied to the car. It's quite a sight to see!

But what happens when the birds travel? Have you ever seen a crow flying along with a suitcase or a hat? That sounds silly, but lots of crows migrate (or go on vacation) in the spring and fall to get away from the bad weather. Some crows fly all the way from Canada in the cold north just to spend a warm winter in Texas.

But how do they fly 50 miles a day on their vacation without even a road map for directions? We're not sure. However, we do know that the crows fly only over the land. Some people think that the crows memorize things along the way and follow the same route every year. That may be true for crows, but what about the ruby-throated hummingbirds that fly across 500 miles of ocean to get from Georgia to Mexico? That means flying continuously day and night without any resting, sleeping, or eating. How do they find their way? Maybe they look at the stars; maybe they have a little compass in their brains. No one knows for sure. However they do it, they migrate without stopping or eating!

Can you imagine a hummingbird carrying a lunch box or maybe a big Mexican hat to keep the hot sun off its head? Those ideas sound silly because we know that God designed these animals so that they wouldn't need to carry along sunglasses, maps, picnic boxes, and hats as we do when we go on a trip.

Although we don't understand all the ways that God provides for His creatures, we do know that God says: *"Look at the crows: they don't plant seeds or gather a harvest; they don't have storage rooms or barns; God feeds them! You are worth so much more than birds!" (Luke 12:24, TEV).*

God loves you. The next time you pack to go on vacation, remember that God has given you talents and skills that are better than any bird has. You can think for yourself. You can choose where you want to go and when. The little hummingbird or the big black crow migrates from place to place because God built the instructions into it. It has little choice. When the weather changes, it gets a feeling that it is time to go. The bird doesn't understand or even care, but just feels that it's time to move on.

God created us different from the animals. We are able to think and choose. However, when God gave us the ability to think and make choices, He also gave us the biggest choice we'll ever make. It is the choice to choose Jesus Christ as our Saviour. Birds and other animals do what they do because God designed them that way. You have a wonderful choice that they don't have. You can accept Jesus Christ! Today is the best day to accept Him into your heart.

In Hot Water!

A minister went on vacation to the seashore and took a stroll along the beach. As he walked he came to a long fishing pier built out into the ocean. It was made of big telephone poles sunk deep into the sand. The poles held up a boardwalk high over the ocean below, like a wooden sidewalk built out over the ocean. People like to walk on the pier and fish from it by leaning over the rail and dropping their lines into the water below.

As the pastor was walking out onto the pier, a lady who was fishing caught his eye. She wasn't using a fishing pole. Instead, she had her line tied to the guardrail. He wondered how she could catch fish with such a rig. His curiosity got the best of him, so he asked her what she was doing.

She smiled and explained that she wasn't trying to catch fish; she was catching blue crabs. Then she explained that down in the water she had a wire basket tied to her line. In the basket, as bait, she had put some chicken parts she had bought at the meat market. She said that the crabs love chicken and will climb right into the basket for a free meal. She explained that she waits patiently until she feels the basket move, then ever so gently she raises the basket with its hungry crabs out of the water. The crabs are so busy eating the chicken dinner that they never notice being lifted from the water.

She told the preacher, "Once I get them out of the water, it's too late for them. I haul up the basket before they can jump out, and I throw them in that bucket over there." She proudly pointed to a white plastic bucket.

The minister went over and looked in at all the confused crabs swimming around and trying desperately to get out. They were about the size of a giant oatmeal cookie and had blue legs and red tipped claws. He turned to the lady and asked one more question: "What do you do with the crabs after you catch them?"

She said, "Oh, I eat them. I take them out of the bucket and drop them into a pot of boiling water to cook."

"Ouch," said the pastor. "What a terrible thing for the crab!"

Then he thought for a moment and said to himself, *You know, that's just what the devil does. First, he lures you into his basket with some sin that you think you would like very much. Then when you least expect it . . . plop! You're in really hot water!*

But there's a way to stay out of hot water! The Bible says: *"The Lord knows how to rescue godly people from their trials"* (2 Peter 2:9, TEV). Godly people are boys and girls who pray to Jesus and do what they know He wants them to do. That's how to stay out of hot water!

Boxer's Fracture

"People with a hot temper do foolish things; wiser people remain calm" (Prov. 14:17, TEV).

Your hands are very complex creations of God. Your hands are so complex that it is hard even to draw a picture of them. If you don't believe me, the next time you watch a cartoon notice how many fingers the characters have. I think you'll find that they usually have just three because it's too hard to draw a hand with four fingers and a thumb and make it look real.

Yes, your hands are a real wonder of God's creation. Now, answer this question as I begin this story: "What do you do with your hands when you fall down?" Don't you put them out in front of you and spread your fingers to catch yourself? You just do it automatically, don't you? You don't make a fist to catch yourself. That would hurt awfully bad when you hit the ground!

Today's story is about a man who told the doctor that he had fallen down and broken a little bone in the side of his hand.

However, the doctor was suspicious, because he knew that a person can't break the little bone the man did unless the fist is closed. So the doctor asked the man to explain how he had fallen down at work. The doctor taped up the man's hand, but really doubted the man was telling the truth. He asked the man again, "Are you *sure* you fell down?"

"Yes, yes," the man replied quite sternly, as if to tell the doctor to mind his own business.

The doctor did his part and left his nurse to finish up and write the accident report. However, just as the man was leaving the office, the doctor asked the man one more time how he hurt his hand. Finally, the man broke down and told the truth. "Doctor," he said, "I

45

was so mad at my boss that I rammed my fist through a wall and broke my hand. I'm so ashamed of what I did that I didn't want anyone to know."

The doctor smiled and said, "I knew you couldn't have broken your hand that way by falling. When we fall down, we spread out our fingers to catch ourselves. The only way you can break that bone is with a closed fist. What happened to you is called a 'boxer's fracture.' It comes from hitting something or somebody with a closed fist."

The doctor was reminded of the proverb written a long time ago that warns: *"If you stay calm, you are wise, but if you have a hot temper, you only show how stupid you are" (Prov. 14:29, TEV).*

Boys and girls, I want to be wise, don't you? Hold up your hands for me and let's do an experiment. Everybody make a fist and then shake hands with the person next to you! Can't do it? All right, let's try it one more time. Everybody open up your fist and shake your neighbor's hand.

What's the lesson here? You can't shake hands and be friendly with a closed fist. Also, you can't get a boxer's fracture with an open and friendly hand.

Puzzled Chickens

"Hold on to instruction, do not let it go; guard it well, for it is your life" (Prov. 4:13, NIV).

Gainesville, Georgia, is called the poultry capital of the world. It seems as though there are chicken houses on every hillside and chicken trucks on every highway. The busy trucks are stacked with cages upon cages of chickens on their way to market. It's not a happy sight if you're a chicken.

However, once in a while some chickens escape from their cages as the delivery truck bumps along the highway. One day I saw three of them standing beside a very busy highway. You'd think that I cheered for the chickens that had found freedom, but I couldn't. The poor things were totally confused and ran around in circles, not knowing what to do next. They had never seen a freeway before. Their world had been life in a long chicken house with 20,000 other chickens. They had never seen an 18-wheeler truck or an automobile. Those chickens were totally unprepared for the world outside of their chicken house. Even if they had turned around and run into the woods, their low intelligence and lack of experience would have only made their chances of being a dinner for a fox that much greater. We were driving on the other side of the road, so I didn't see what happened to them, but I can only think the worst.

Many times young people start out in life in a way similar to falling from a chicken truck. They are not prepared for the real world. I suppose chickens will never learn reading, writing, and arithmetic, but boys and girls do. In addition, boys and girls can grow up to be missionaries, doctors, electricians, teachers, preachers, nurses, firefighters, and lots of other great things. A chicken usually grows up to be somebody's dinner.

God made the chicken, and He also made you. A chicken has no choice about what it will grow up to be, but you can be anything you want to be. Of course, you have to stay in school and learn all you can so that God can best use you. A Bible proverb says that you should hold on to instruction, not let it go, and guard it well. We would say today, "Get all of the training you can. Anything less is just jumping off the truck!"

Cowbirds

The cowbird is like a bad habit. I'll explain why after I tell you a little bit about cowbirds. The trail herders and cowboys of long ago used to call them buffalo birds because they waddled along behind the buffalo herds. Today most of the buffalo are gone, so we just call them cowbirds.

Cowbirds never raise their own babies. Instead, they lay their eggs in nests of other birds that are often smaller than they are. But they don't always get away with their little trick. Robins and catbirds throw their eggs out, and some birds just bury their eggs by building a new nest. These birds don't want the cowbird eggs to hatch for a very good reason. Cowbird chicks are very selfish.

However, many birds never notice the cowbird eggs mixed in with their own eggs. When the cowbird chicks hatch, they are often bigger than the others in the nest, and the larger cowbird chicks often throw the other birds out of the nest so that they can have all the food for themselves. Then after they're grown up, they leave the nest without even a thank you to the birds that raised them.

Cowbird chicks are a lot like the bad habits of people. If you let a bad habit get into your nest, it outgrows your good habits and throws them out. The devil puts the bad eggs into your nest, and it's up to you to throw them out!

There's an example found in Luke 11 about the danger of throwing out bad habits and not replacing them with good ones. Jesus warned that if the bad spirit was not replaced, it would return with seven others that were even worse. We need to replace our bad habits with good habits from Jesus. Learning your Bible and studying your lessons are good habits from Jesus.

Being kind to other young people and freely sharing your things are good habits. Obeying your parents or the people who take care of you is a good habit. So is coming to church every week and learning more about Jesus. Let's always pray that our lives will be full of good habits that come from Jesus!

Alternate Version for Young Children

Cowbird babies are like some kids I have known. I'll explain why after I tell you a little bit about cowbirds. The trail herders and cowboys of long ago used to call them buffalo birds because they waddled along behind the buffalo herds. Today the buffalo are almost all gone, so we just call them cowbirds.

Cowbirds never raise their own babies. Instead, they lay their eggs in the nests of other birds that are often smaller than they are. But they don't always get away with their little trick. Robins and catbirds throw their eggs out, and some birds just bury their eggs by building a new nest. Birds don't want the cowbird eggs to hatch for a very good reason. Cowbird chicks are very selfish.

Many birds never notice the cowbird eggs mixed in with their own eggs. When the cowbird chicks hatch, they are often bigger than the others in the nest. The larger cowbird chicks frequently eat all the food for themselves. Then after they are grown up, they leave the nest without even saying thank you to the birds that raised them.

I think we all know people who act just like a cowbird baby. They always want more than their share, and they talk loudly and shove themselves ahead of everyone else. Sometimes they are like that for a reason. Maybe what they really want is attention or someone to love them.

You know what you can do? You can tell them about Jesus. He loves all girls and boys whether they act like cowbirds or not!

Stay by the Post

When Marvin was growing up in Ohio, he lived on the edge of town—almost in the country. A couple of miles from his house was a small dairy farm. Two brothers had a herd of cows and their own milk delivery route. They milked the cows and pasteurized and bottled their own milk. The milk was poured into glass bottles, and little paper stoppers were snapped in the top to seal them. One of the brothers drove their little white milk truck and made deliveries very early in the morning, before the people in the town got up. He would pick up the empty bottles off the porch and leave fresh bottles of milk. Marvin liked to visit their dairy farm and help wherever he could.

One day after school Marvin rode his bicycle to the dairy farm. Sometimes he would just hang around, and sometimes he would help bring in the cows for the evening milking. (Cows are milked twice a day.) Well, that afternoon Marvin was just hanging around when he heard one of the cows making an awful noise out in the pasture. She kept mooing and mooing and wouldn't stop. The farmer heard it too and was worried about what was going on.

Marvin went with him to find out what was wrong. They left the barnyard, climbed the pasture fence, and started walking toward the mooing cow. They had walked for quite a ways before the farmer spotted the cow that was making all the noise. When he saw her, he realized that this was a cow that had recently had a calf. He also figured out that she probably had lost her calf somewhere and was calling for it.

Now, any farmer will tell you that cows are not very smart. They are among the least intelligent of all farm animals. So when the cow saw Marvin and the farmer, not being too smart, she must have

51

thought, *My baby is missing, and they took it!* Being angry, she put her head down and charged.

Not needing further instructions, Marvin and the farmer turned and ran for the fence. They jumped over the fence, and Marvin took off running. That's when the farmer yelled after Marvin to come back and stand next to the fence post where he was.

Out in the field the cow was mooing, pawing the ground, and threatening to charge. Marvin thought that the smart thing was to run as far and as fast as he could, but the farmer knew better. However, Marvin followed the farmer's instructions and came back and knelt with him behind the fence post. Then the farmer told Marvin to stay by the post, because if the cow charged through the fence, they could climb over and get on the other side. The farmer said not to leave the post, because the cow wouldn't charge through it!

Marvin and the farmer knelt there by the post as the farmer talked in quiet tones to the cow. Although cows don't really understand English, she finally figured out that they didn't have her baby and left to find her calf. Eventually the cow found her baby, and Marvin learned a good lesson. When you are in trouble, stay by something solid. It's foolish to try to outrun trouble. Instead, stay by what your mom and dad or guardian teaches you. Listen to your elders. Go with what you know, and don't go running off on your own.

Bad Language

"Do not use my name for evil purposes, because I, the Lord your God, will punish anyone who misuses my name" (Ex. 20:7, TEV).

Bad habits are easy to make and hard to break. A bad habit some young people have is using bad language.

One very early spring Marv went to visit his grandpa's farm during lambing time. Grandpa had lots of lambs in the barn and even several in the house. Two of the lambs were sick, so Grandma had them in a box in the dining room and fed them with a baby bottle. This was the first time Marv saw a real lamb's tail. He didn't know that lambs are born with long woolly tails. Did you? He thought lambs come into the world with little stubs for tails. They don't.

That spring he found out that for health reasons sheep have their tails cut off soon after they are born. A long woolly tail is hard for the sheep to keep clean. In fact, they are very nasty if left to grow. So for the good health of the animal the farmer cuts it off.

Marv's grandpa let him watch as he used his special cutter and the dark medicine that he dabbed on the cut after he was finished. In one swift action the tail was cut off, the pain was over, and in a few days the lamb healed up and forgot that it ever had a long tail. Cutting off the long tail helped the lamb stay healthy. Even though the lamb didn't know it, it was worth the pain.

But I can't help wondering if there would have been a better way. Wouldn't it have been kinder to the lamb to cut off its tail in little pieces at a time instead of one big cut? Wouldn't it be better to have a lot of little pains instead of one big one? Of course, you're already ahead of me. Every piece cut off of the lamb's tail would hurt all the same. My idea of a bunch of little cuts is silly!

So I wonder about people and using bad language. We call it

cussing, swearing, profanity, taking the Lord's name in vain, or just being nasty-mouthed. I wonder if a person wanted to stop using bad language, would it be better to stop cussing just a little at a time? Or would it be better to say that from this day on you'll stop doing it? In a way the use of bad language is like hurting Jesus one word at a time. Every time you say a bad word, you hurt Him and yourself a little.

The Bible says: *"No bad language must pass your lips, but only what is good and helpful to the occasion, so that it brings a blessing to those who hear it" (Eph. 4:29, NEB).*

Today pray to Jesus if you have the bad habit of cussing so that you will be able to throw it on the pile of "lamb's tail" habits. Then never pick it up again.

Eating Dates in the Dark

Have you ever heard the story about a nomad who woke up hungry one night in his desert tent? The story says that he had a bowl of dates near his bed, so he lit a candle to see his midnight snack. He reached into the bowl and pulled out a big juicy date and held it up to the flickering light. But in the candlelight he saw a worm wiggling out of the fruit, so he tossed the date away. He reached into the bowl a second time, and his mouth watered as he held the date up to the candle. Another worm! He tossed the second date and reached for a third. The light from the candle revealed yet another worm squirming in a hole. In disgust the nomad threw the date away and blew out the candle. The story says that he ate the rest of the dates in the dark, worms and all!

Eating dates in the dark is like what the Bible calls a dead conscience. It means that you don't have any feelings left, so you don't care. I had a teacher once who had lost all feeling on one side of his body because he got hurt in a war. He explained to us that he could hold his hand over a flame, and it wouldn't ever hurt. He told us that he could cut himself or hit his finger with a hammer, and it would never ache. It sounded so good. No more pain!

But there was another side to his story. He explained that there had been times when he had burned himself and never known it until he smelled his skin burning! He had no feeling, so if he accidentally cut himself, he might not find out until he was in serious trouble. He had no warning that he was hurting himself until it was too late.

That's the way it is with a dead conscience. You can hurt yourself very badly before you realize what you have done. The Bible tells us about "deceitful liars, whose consciences are dead, as if burnt with a hot iron" (1 Tim. 4:2, TEV). Our conscience is that little warning voice that tells us to be careful or we may get burned.

This can be the case with drugs. Playing with drugs is like the nomad who blew out the candle. You know they are not good for you. You know they are full of worms, but like the man in the parable, you blow out the light and ignore your conscience. The nomad got a belly full of worms, but drugs are much worse.

Your best protection is your conscience when Jesus is in control of it. If your conscience says don't do it, then don't do it! Don't blow out the candle!

The Bulldozer
and the Train Wreck

"Obey your leaders and follow their orders" (Heb. 13:17, TEV).

From time to time the railroad has to put down new tracks to replace the worn out ones. The new rails are often so long that they are hauled on a special rail train. Each rail can be a quarter mile long! That means four of them laid end to end would stretch for a full mile. That's a long rail! These trains have to be loaded at the steel mill where the rail is made. Rail trains are made up of a line of flat cars pulled by several engines. The new rails look like long steel ribbons of silver spaghetti laid out on rollers on the open cars.

It all began when a fully loaded rail train was traveling a track from Georgia to South Carolina. Up ahead, beside the same railroad track, a man was running a bulldozer that had a big bush cutter. The cutter looked like a giant lawn mower on a long arm. The man's job was to drive his bulldozer along and cut the bushes away from the sides of the track. Everything was going well until the man had to cross the tracks to cut bushes on the other side. He was supposed to park his bulldozer, walk to his truck, drive to the nearest phone, and call the train people to get permission to cross the tracks. They would tell him when the next train was to come through. But he thought that going to so much trouble took too much time. Instead, he decided to go ahead and drive across without telling anybody. Who would ever know?

Now, where he was working there were two sets of railroad tracks with a little ditch in the center between them. The little ditch was just wide enough so that trains could pass going in opposite directions and deep enough to keep water from washing over the tracks. Being very careful, the man looked and listened for a train . . . and then started across. The bulldozer bellowed black smoke and nosed down into the ditch. Everything was just fine until it started up the other side. The bush cutter arm on the back of the dozer got caught on the track! The cutter arm wedged between the tracks, and the dozer lost its grip and began to spin its big tracks in the gravel. It was hung fast and couldn't move backward or forward. The man tried and tried to get the dozer loose. Time passed, and then suddenly he heard the rail train coming!

What happened after that was terrible. The train plowed into the bulldozer and wrecked. All the rails bent into long cold snakes of steel. The locomotives fell off the track and caught fire. The new rails that the train was hauling were so bent that they had to be cut in pieces to be removed.

It was the next day before they found the bulldozer driver hiding in a nearby motel. He was afraid to come out and hear what had happened.

In some ways I can feel sorry for the man, because he was doing his job. He was even so ambitious that he didn't want to wait around for someone to give him clearance. I'm sure he thought everything would be all right. Probably he had done it many times before. But this time when he didn't listen to instructions, a terrible thing happened.

I think if we were to ask him today if he learned a lesson, he would tell us *always* to obey the rules. Yes, even grown-ups must obey rules.

Furthermore, the Bible says: *"Children, it is your Christian duty to obey your parents, for this is the right thing to do" (Eph. 6:1, TEV).* We too must always obey the rules, because they are there for our own good.

Flying by Faith

How many of you have flown in an airplane? If you have, then you probably flew into some clouds. That can be a really scary experience because you can't see where you are going or where you are. Some pilots have become so confused in clouds that they have flown upside down while thinking they were right side up! That can really happen, and here's how I found out about it.

Just for fun I took some flying lessons in a small single-engine plane. In my training I learned that there were lots of instruments to tell me what was going on while I was flying the plane. One instrument showed how high up I was, another how fast I was going, and another how much gas I had left. These instruments were all very important, but one was especially important. It's called an artificial horizon. It kind of looks like a little computer screen with an airplane in it. It showed me if I was in what pilots call straight and level flight. That's especially important information to know when flying into a cloud.

Flying inside a cloud is like driving in a fog, except for one thing—there's no road underneath you. Everything all around you is just mist. You can't see up, down, or sideways. Now, down here on earth people driving cars find it easy to get around because they can follow the road and keep between the lines. But up there in the sky there are no yellow and white lines. There are no road signs or traffic signals. And most of all, you can't just pull over and stop!

It's easy to get into trouble flying in clouds. Without the special instrument, you don't know if you're diving toward the earth or climbing toward the sun. That may sound silly, but it's very easy to get confused when your eyes can't see which way is up. When flying in a cloud, you have to trust your instruments. You can't trust your feelings because you can easily become confused and think the plane is climbing when it is really diving to the earth. It has happened a lot of times, and the result is often a plane crash. You must trust the instruments to be safe. Even if you don't agree with what the instrument says, you must not fly the plane by how you feel. You must have faith in your instruments.

The very same thing is true in this Christian life. We need to have faith that Jesus loves us and that He will always watch over us. If you get up in the morning feeling lower than a snake's belly in a wagon track, you still should live that day by faith and not by how you feel. The clouds may seem to be all around you. Your friends may be mad at you. Your teacher may look at you wrong. Perhaps nobody pays any attention to you. In such times you need to remind yourself to keep your eye on Jesus and go on by faith, remembering that on the other side of the clouds the sun will always shine again.

"For our life is a matter of faith, not of sight" (2 Cor. 5:7, TEV).

The Frog Pond of Your Heart

"A man that hath friends must shew himself friendly" (Prov. 18:24).
Franklin was fascinated by little outdoor goldfish ponds. He'd
seen one for the first time when he was in elementary school. He was
walking home one afternoon when he looked through a wooden
fence and saw a little pond made of rocks and cement. It was filled
with fancy goldfish lazily swimming in the afternoon sun. It was really neat. He knew right then and there that he wanted his own goldfish pond! He planned to put a little fountain in it, fill it with all
kinds of goldfish, and then have it ruled over by one big frog.

The time finally came when he built his own goldfish pond. It
was small, about the size of a kid's plastic wading pool. For plants
Franklin went to a farm pond about a mile away and got some lily
pads and other water plants. In the center of the pond he placed some
big stones so that the birds could land and drink there. All around the
outside he planted special border grass for decoration and as a home
for bugs and insects that the fish would eat. One of the last things he
had to do was build a fence around it to keep his German shepherd
dog from using the fish pond as a bathtub.

Finally the day came when he stocked it with goldfish. It was almost perfect. The fish loved their new home, and Franklin enjoyed
watching them swim around the lily pads and turn lazy circles in the
fresh clean water.

It wasn't long before a snake doctor (you might call them drag-
onflies) showed up to hover over the pond and investigate. Then
along came birds to drink and bathe, and colorful butterflies to suck
on the plants' sweet juices.

As I said, it was almost perfect. But one thing was still missing a
big green frog! Franklin wanted a frog to rule over his pond, so he

61

asked a friend how to attract one. The friend told Franklin that the chances of attracting a frog would be really good if he had everything that a frog would like. He said he didn't know how frogs found out about things like new ponds, but somehow they got the word.

As the weeks went by, Franklin's little pond took on a life of its own. The goldfish stopped eating the food the he sprinkled on the water because they found plenty of natural food. The plants grew, and the water turned crystal clear. His little pond kingdom was in nature's balance, except for a frog. But he had been told that if he made things just right, a frog would come.

Well, one morning when Franklin walked by his little pond, he was surprised to hear the unmistakable plunk of a frog jumping into the water. Not believing his ears, Franklin waited quietly to see if two little eyes would pop up to the surface the way frogs do. And then . . . and then . . . sure enough, a little green frog surfaced in the pond! It was just a little fellow, about the size of a chicken egg, but it sure looked pretty sitting on the rock in the center of the goldfish pond. Franklin's pond kingdom was complete.

The Bible says that if you want to have friends, you have to show yourself friendly. Maybe we could say that our lives are like goldfish ponds. If we plant kindness and happiness and other good things in our lives, we will attract things that are beautiful, such as good friends. If you prepare for them, they will come. Let's every one of us put a little goldfish pond of beauty in our hearts and attract others for Jesus.

Groundhog in a Tree!

Birds are found on tree branches, and groundhogs are found in burrows in the ground . . . most of the time. One day Judy visited her parents in the country. They lived at the end of a long lane that went through the woods and up a hill to their house. As she drove through the woods she heard her dad's dogs barking like crazy. The dogs were named Bubbles, Felix, Sparky, and Smokey. Judy stopped the car and looked out the window to see what all of the noise was about. That's when she saw the dogs under a tree, and they were barking and running in circles. They kept looking up and jumping at something in the tree.

Bubbles, the boxer dog, was the biggest, loudest, and scariest. Felix, Sparky, and Smokey were all little dogs with barks bigger than their bites. The dogs continued howling as Judy tried to find out what they were barking at. And finally she saw it. There was a groundhog way up in the tree! Up high in a fork where two branches divided sat a furry groundhog, and it was holding on with its front paws for all it was worth. Judy could see its black eyes shining with fear because of the dogs below. Actually, the groundhog could have easily held its own with the little dogs, but the big dog was many times its size.

Now, I suppose you know that groundhogs don't live in trees. They live in dens under the ground that are connected with tunnels and several entrances. When something tries to get them, they dash into their holes and disappear deep into the ground. It is Judy's best guess that this groundhog must have been munching on some fresh flowers or grass and gotten caught away from those escape holes. It looked like the animal had decided that if you can't go down, then go up. So it made a dash for safety up the nearest tree. Judy said it was a pitiful sight to see a little groundhog in a big tree surrounded by those vicious dogs. I'm sure that the groundhog planned to hold on and that it hoped the dogs would lose interest. Maybe it would even sneak down the tree after it got dark.

However, there is one thing the groundhog didn't know that Judy did. The frightened animal was perfectly safe. You see, what Judy knew that the treed animal didn't was that the big dog, called Bubbles, was so old that she didn't have any teeth! Bubbles looked scary and made a lot of noise, but had no teeth!

Boys and girls, that's the way it is when the devil gets after you. Because you have Jesus protecting you, the devil can huff and puff and scare you, but he doesn't have any teeth. Jesus has already won the fight with the devil. That's why the Bible says: *"Resist the Devil, and he will run away from you. Come near to God, and he will come near to you" (James 4:7, 8, TEV).* And also in Revelation 12:12 it says: *"For the Devil has come down to you, and he is filled with rage, because he knows that he has only a little time left" (TEV).*

Remember, Jesus protects you because when you give your life to Him, the devil has no teeth!

Grandpa's Gourds

Every year during the Thanksgiving season Sam's grandpa would place baskets of brightly colored gourds on his dining room table. Some looked like miniature pumpkins, and others were covered with bright colors and stripes. You can buy them in the supermarket today, but Sam's grandpa grew his own. He had a special place by his garden fence where he planted a few gourd seeds every year. During the summer the vines would climb the fence, and by fall it was hanging full of beautiful gourds of all shapes and colors. Sam loved his grandpa's gourds.

One spring Sam decided to plant some gourds of his own. He bought a pack of seeds and anxiously waited for the ground to get warm enough to plant. Just before school was out for the summer, he dug up a little place by his backyard fence. After carefully preparing the soil, he used one of his mom's tablespoons for a shovel and planted the gourd seeds in a little hill. Then he waited for them to come up. Finally, one day the shoots started pushing up through the soil. Sam was thrilled as he faithfully carried water in a quart jar to the tiny little plants.

He imagined what it would look like to see his fence hanging with colorful gourds. All sorts of plans ran through his head. He would dry some and make water dippers out of them so that he could drink cool water down at the spring. Maybe he would take a bigger one and cut out a hole to make a bird house. There were just lots of things he was going to do once the gourds got grown. But the summer came, and Sam got busy playing. School was out, and he neglected the gourds. The weather turned hot, and the little plants got thirsty. Now and then Sam would water his plants in the evening. But he got busier and busier, and so he watered his plants less and less. When he would run past his little gourd plants, he'd say to himself, "Sometime I'm going to have to water those plants. I'll do it this evening when it gets cooler." Of course, when the evening came, Sam said that he would water them sometime in the morning.

By now you can guess what happened. Sam's gourds died of thirst. They just dried up and perished from neglect. I suppose we should call him Sometime Sam, because he was always going to water the plants "sometime." When the fall came, all that Sometime Sam had left was a little dry spot by the fence.

What did Sometime Sam do wrong? He really *did* want the gourds to grow. He really *did* intend to water them, but he just never got around to doing what he said he was going to do . . . sometime.

When I think of Sometime Sam's dried up plants, I think of a letter that Preacher Paul of the Bible wrote to a young pastor named Timothy. He told Timothy how to be a good servant of Jesus. He told him not to neglect the special gift that God had given him. Timothy's gift was preaching, but you might have a gift of teaching, or the heart of a missionary or doctor or nurse. These gifts are like tender little plants that need your special care. They can't be treated like Sam treated his gourds, or they will also dry up and die.

By the way, a few years later Sometime Sam planted some more gourds. This time he was older and wiser. He watered and cared for them, and was rewarded with gourds so colorful that they looked like a fence full of Christmas decorations. So maybe now we should change Sometime Sam's name to Every Time Sam, because he learned his lesson.

Whatever the gift that God gives you—and everyone has a special gift—remember to take care of it, and you will grow to be something beautiful in God's garden.

Raking Hay
While the Sun Shines

"You may be sure that your sin will find you out" (Num. 32: 23, NIV).

City Boy Sam's aunts and uncles were farmers in Ohio. They raised cows, pigs, and chickens along with a few cats and dogs, and a couple of ponies. Since all these animals eat lots of food, the farmers also grew corn, wheat, and oats, and they baled hay to feed and bed down their animals in the winter.

Every year after school was out, City Boy Sam would go to spend the summer with his cousins on the farm. Oh, how he wanted to drive the tractor, but he was always too young!

One summer during hay baling time, City Boy Sam's uncle took Sam out to a field of long grass that had been mowed the day before. (A baling machine squeezes the dried grass into heavy bundles and ties strings around them. When the dried bundle of grass is spit out the back of the baling machine, it's called a bale of hay, which the farmer can use to feed the animals during the winter.) The long grass was all lying flat on the ground, drying in the sun.

But City Boy Sam's uncle discovered that he was one person short of having enough people to do the job, so he decided that he would trust City Boy Sam to drive the tractor that pulled the hay rake. The hay rake was a machine that was pulled along behind the tractor. It piled the hay in long low rows. All Sam had to do was to drive around and around the field in giant circles and let the hay rake make the rows.

Sam's uncle rode around with him several times to make sure that Sam understood just how it was done. When he was satisfied that City Boy Sam knew what to do, he set the gas feed and told Sam not to go any faster. He explained that if the tractor went too fast, the rake would make the pile too high, and the baler would choke up and not be able to make the bales. When his uncle left, Sam was excited finally to be on his own.

He drove around and around, with the tractor going *putt, putt, putt.* Time after time Sam drove around the field, and it got more and more boring. You already know what he did next, don't you? Yes, Sam speeded up the tractor just a little bit. Everything worked fine, so he speeded it up some more. The hay rake just kept right on piling the grass higher and higher. It was fun as the tractor bumped along faster and faster. Before Sam knew it, the job was all done. No more grass to rake. So he got off the tractor and went to visit his uncle in the next field and tell him the good news. Uncle looked surprised at the news and walked back with Sam to look over his work.

Uncle looked disappointed and didn't need to ask if City Boy Sam had speeded up the tractor. When they looked at the rows, it was plain that they had gotten higher and higher and higher as Sam had driven faster and faster. Needless to say, Uncle was unhappy with City Boy Sam, because what Sam had done would make everyone's work harder. That afternoon every time the hay baler choked, so did Sam.

As the Bible says, Sam's sin had found him out (Num. 32:23). His disobedience was piled in long rows all around the field. Thankfully Sam's uncle was a kindly man, so he slowed the baler a little and was able to finish the work without too much trouble.

City Boy Sam was truly sorry. He didn't clearly understand what would happen if he pulled the hay rake too fast. After seeing what he had done, he apologized, and his uncle forgave him. That's the way Jesus forgives us when we sin. If we're truly sorry and ask Him to forgive us, He will. The Bible says: *"If we confess our sins to God, he will keep his promise and do what is right: he will forgive us our sins and purify us from all our wrongdoing" (1 John 1:9, TEV).*

What Goes Up
Must Come Down!

"A good reputation is better than expensive perfume" *(Eccl. 7:1, TEV).*

When little Frankie was in middle school, he had a class called penmanship that teaches kids to write in longhand. The teacher passed out old-fashioned ink pens and little bottles of deep blue ink. For an hour a week the students would carefully write between the lines, forming perfect letters with real pens and ink. The ink was indelible, which means you can't wash it out of your clothes or off your hands. You had to let it wear off.

Because of the mess of keeping little bottles of ink in the desks, the teacher collected them after penmanship class and stored them in a cabinet at the front of the room. She also kept several big bottles of ink to refill the smaller inkwells.

One morning when little Frankie got to school, everyone was upset. Someone had broken into the school during the night and vandalized it. Papers were thrown on the floor, desks were turned over, the principal's office was a mess, and worst of all, someone had thrown ink all over the walls and ceiling of the classroom. The place was a mess!

Frankie's teacher looked pretty grim that morning. She was sad that someone would break into the school, and angry because of what they had done to the room. After the opening bell, all the students were told to remain in their seats and wait for the principal to come to the class. The students were scared because they didn't know what he might do. It was a big school, and it took a long time for the principal to go from room to room. Finally the door swung open, and in he walked . . . with a police officer. The principal told the students to place their hands on top of their desks. Then he and the police officer walked up and down every row, looking at the backs and palms of the students' hands. Why do you suppose they did that? Well, the principal said that what goes up must come down, so whoever threw the ink up on the ceiling would have it on his or her hands.

Little Frankie and his classmates were relieved, because everyone in their classroom had clean hands! But some older boys down the hall did not. The ink wouldn't wash off, and they were caught and punished. After that, even though the ink had worn off, they were known as the kids who threw the ink. The ink wore off their hands, but their reputation did not disappear.

The Bible says that a good reputation is better than expensive perfume. Here again, the perfume washes off, but a good reputation stays. There is only one way to have a lasting, good reputation— always ask yourself one simple question before you do something you are not sure about. Ask yourself what Jesus would do if He were in your place. Doing what Jesus would do will always give you a good reputation. You'll never have to worry about trying to wash off the ink of bad deeds!

Yes, do what Jesus would do!

Jason and the Rifle

"My dear brothers, take note of this: Everyone should be quick to listen, slow to speak and slow to become angry" (James 1:19, NIV)

Jason and his friend were out in the yard playing with a .22 caliber rifle after school. It was before most people got home from work, so the neighborhood was quiet. Jason's parents were also at work, and he was not allowed to shoot his gun in town.

Even though a .22 is one of the smallest rifles made, the bullet can still travel a full mile through the air before it lands. Jason's gun and all other guns are dangerous and can kill people!

Jason was pointing his rifle and pretending to shoot at his neighbor's house when his buddy dared him to actually shoot the gun. He dared Jason to shoot out an electrical socket in the neighbor's carport. It was just across the yard, and it made such an inviting target! Jason must have thought it was all right to shoot, because it was only a little piece of plastic and some metal. It couldn't cost much. And besides, it looked like such a good target.

Jason knew better, but his buddy called him a chicken. Now, nobody wants to be a chicken, and neither did Jason. He played with the idea of shooting the socket. Because the people were not at home, he aimed the rifle, pretended he was going to shoot, and then he stopped and grinned at his friend. Jason kept pretending until . . . before he knew what had happened, the gun went off accidentally with a loud bang. The socket exploded. Two really scared boys ran for the house and put up the rifle, and they promised each other never to tell what happened.

A few days later the neighbor asked Jason's dad if he had seen anyone shooting guns around the neighborhood. The man was upset because a bullet had shot out his electrical socket, passed through the kitchen cabinet, crashed through the china closet, and stuck in their living room wall. The little bullet had done lots and lots of damage.

Eventually Jason confessed, but you don't want to hear about his punishment. Instead, let's talk for a moment about what went on in his mind before he pulled the trigger. He never dreamed that the rifle bullet could do that much damage. He never dreamed of hurting his neighbors' property, because he liked the people and they liked him. He just didn't think about what might happen.

Sometimes the words we use are like rifle bullets that do a lot more damage than we ever meant. Making fun of people because of their skin color or because they wear glasses or if they are fat or skinny, smart or not, are all rifle shots into another person's heart. You cannot take back the words you speak once they are said, just as Jason couldn't put the bullet back in his gun. Once it's done, you have to live with what you said. And like the bullet, the damage may not seem like much on the surface, but it's the damage that you can't see that's so severe. It's the inside hurt that you don't see that really matters.

The Bible tells us that we should be like Jesus—quick to listen, slow to speak, and very careful and considerate of others. I want always to talk and act like Jesus, don't you?

How to Be a Better Television Watcher

I have a grown-up friend who used to be a television junkie. He would sit down in front of the TV and wouldn't move until the last program went off at night. He didn't even like most of the programs, but once he got in front of the TV, he couldn't get up. He said he was so helpless that he couldn't even get up to change the channels. If cartoons came on, he watched cartoons; if some trashy show came on, he watched it. He was helpless in front of his television!

My friend got a guilty conscience. What he was doing bothered him because he was a Christian and knew better. He started worrying about how embarrassing it would be if the neighbors dropped in when something bad was on TV. He also worried that if you watch something long enough, you begin to like it. It's like hanging around with a bad crowd. If you hang out with them long enough, you even begin to act like them. You talk like them, you walk like them, and you start to think like them. He knew that what was happening to him wasn't good.

In his heart he wanted to think, talk, and act like Jesus. He often thought about a saying by the fisherman Peter: *"A person is a slave of anything that has conquered him" (2 Peter 2:19, TEV)*. My friend was becoming a slave to television. It had conquered him, and he knew it! He didn't want to keep filling his mind with trashy stuff, so can you guess what he did? He unplugged his TV and took it out and sold it! That solved his problem, and to this day he's not a slave to television. Good for him! He's a happy man.

But as for me, I think selling the TV set is not necessary for most people. My friend is happier today without a television, so for him it was a good idea. However, we aren't all like him. What about the

73

rest of us? I like to watch TV, and probably you do too. But how much television can we watch and still follow the directions given to us in the Bible: *"Fill your minds with those things that are good and that deserve praise: things that are true, noble, right, pure, lovely and honorable" (Phil. 4:8, TEV).* How can we do this and still enjoy a little TV now and then?

I have a simple solution that will give you a good start. All you have to do is put a picture on top of your television set. However, I'm not talking about a picture of your favorite baseball player or movie star. Instead, I'm suggesting that you place a picture on your TV of Someone whose presence will always affect what you watch in a good way. For better watching, why not put a picture of *Jesus* on top of your television and see what a difference it makes?

The Sticky Tree

George came from a faraway country called Lebanon and had recently moved to America. He was a man with coal black hair, deep black eyes, and a tiny mustache. He grew up on a farm in the nation of Lebanon, which is not far from where Jesus lived when He was a boy. George's home country is warm and beautiful, with a long shoreline on the Mediterranean Sea. It lies under a migration route for birds. Hundreds of thousands of birds fly over Lebanon every spring and again every fall on their way from their summer and winter homes. A migration route or flyway is like a big invisible highway in the sky. We are not sure how the birds know how to fly the long distances they do, but we do know that they take the same route year after year . . . and without a map! This is a story about those migrating birds and what happened to some of them.

When George was a boy, his uncle taught him how to catch wild songbirds. He caught all sorts of birds and kept them because of their beauty and their pretty songs. They lived in cages all around the house. He said that they had a whole roomful of birds in cages just to look at and listen to. But some of them also tasted good!

Now, let's stop here for a minute. In the United States it's against the law to trap songbirds, and it's really gross to think of someone eating them. But George came from another country with different laws and customs. We here in the United States would not think of trapping and eating robins, cardinals, and mockingbirds, would we? It's against the law.

Well anyway, every spring and fall thousands and thousands of brightly colored European finches would fly over where George lived. They're brown birds with bright red faces and throats, and a broad yellow band across their black wings. George wanted to catch some, but they were too high up in the sky, so here's what his uncle taught him. George would go to a hilltop and strip all the leaves off a small tree. Next he would take a super-sticky mixture of sugar and honey and spread it all over the branches. Then he would go back to the house and get his caged birds and put them under the sticky tree.

Can you guess what happened next? The birds in the cages would sing, and the birds flying over would hear them and come down to see what all of the singing was about. When they landed on the branches, the glue-like mixture would stick their feet in place and hold them until George could catch them. By now you've figured out what happened to the captured birds.

Sometimes the devil does something just like that to us. He uses other people, sometimes even our friends, to try to get us to do something we would not normally do. They tell us to join them—just like the birds in the cages under the tree. But when we give in to temptation to do wrong, we're stuck! Only Jesus can free us, and only by obeying Jesus in the first place can we always be safe. When someone calls to you and tries to get you to do something wrong, don't go. Don't get stuck!

Land Mines in France

"We, however, are citizens of heaven, and we eagerly wait for our Savior, the Lord Jesus Christ, to come from heaven. He will change our weak mortal bodies and make them like his own glorious body" (Phil. 3:20, 21, TEV).

Aunt Inga creaked when she walked. It was her knee. She had a wooden leg with a squeaky knee. When I first met her, I would have never guessed she had a wooden leg if someone hadn't told me. But if you watched very carefully as she walked, you could see that she had a slight limp. Aunt Inga was really good at using her wooden leg. After she put a sock and shoe on it, I'm sure most people never even noticed it was false.

However, I want to tell you the sad story about why she had to wear an artificial leg.

Aunt Inga was a little French girl growing up during World War II. Beside the roads of her country the enemy had hidden little bombs called antipersonnel mines. These little bombs have triggers on them something like a mousetrap. They snap when you step on them, and then the bomb explodes. The little mine is not meant to kill you. Instead, it's meant to ruin a leg or a foot. They are mean and cruel weapons that still blow up people . . . even today.

Well, the story I'm telling you happened a long time ago when Aunt Inga was just a little girl who didn't understand about war or little bombs buried in the woods. So one day she walked with her family from one village to another to visit her grandma. Inga was young and impatient because the old folks walked so slowly. As she ran ahead, her mother would yell to her, "Don't get off of the road! Don't run into the woods! It's not safe in the woods."

But little Inga wouldn't listen. She was bored. Besides, she thought, who would know if she ran into the woods or not? So when she got out of sight of her parents, she darted into the woods to pick some flowers.

You can guess the rest. Inga stepped on one of these hidden bombs, and it blew up, leaving her there screaming with a badly hurt foot and leg. Of course, the next problem was how to get her out and not have her parents also get blown up. Somehow they rescued her without getting hurt. They wrapped a handkerchief around her hurt leg and carried her to a hospital. Her foot and leg were hurt too badly to save. Because of her disobedience, today Aunt Inga walks around on a squeaky wooden leg, but she doesn't let it slow her down. She's a happy lady who always has a big friendly smile.

Aunt Inga is happy because she's a Christian who is looking forward to running to meet Jesus in heaven. She knows that Jesus has promised that heaven will have no sick or crippled people. The Bible says that in heaven God will *"wipe away all tears from their eyes. There will be no more death, no more grief or crying or pain. The old things have disappeared"* (Rev. 21:4, TEV).

Won't that be great? Aunt Inga thinks so!

Story 6

Look-alikes

Some people like to dress up and put on wigs and makeup so that they look just like someone else. They are called impersonators. To them this may be fun, but many animals are look-alikes for much more serious reasons.

If a mockingbird tries to eat a monarch butterfly, the bird is in for a real surprise. After the first bite, the mockingbird thinks that it has just bitten into the sourest lemon it has ever tasted. The butterfly tastes so bad that it makes the mockingbird throw up! The bird immediately spits out the butterfly and remembers never to try to eat any more butterflies that look like a monarch! Of course, this is the way that the monarch butterfly protects itself.

However, in God's creation there is another butterfly that mockingbirds also won't eat, even though it would taste good to the bird. This is because it is a monarch butterfly look-alike, a butterfly that lives on the monarch's reputation. It's called the viceroy, which means "in place of the king." The viceroy butterfly looks very similar to the king of butterflies, the monarch. The big difference between the two butterflies is that the monarch is bad-tasting and the viceroy isn't. However, when a bird sees a viceroy, it thinks of the bad-tasting monarch and leaves the other one alone. The viceroy protects itself by looking like the monarch. A viceroy is a look-alike on the outside, but inside it's different—it's a viceroy.

Butterflies are not the only look-alikes. Sometimes people try to be someone they are not. Have you ever tried to fool someone by trying to look like someone else? I knew a boy who tried it when he visited Germany. He wanted to look like a German so that he could blend in, so he bought new German clothes and shoes. When he got all dressed up, he looked just like a German. No one could tell the difference. That is, no one could tell until he had to talk. When he tried to speak his broken German, everyone instantly knew from his accent that he was an American. He was a good German look-alike on the outside, but inside he was very much an American. He was trying to be something he was not, and those who know better easily found him out.

Of course, the lesson here is that we can look and act like something we are not. We can become look-alikes and fool most of the people some of the time. But like the viceroy butterfly, we are living on someone else's reputation.

Indeed, Christian boys and girls should try to be look-alikes—looking like Jesus. When people see us, they are to see Jesus inside of us. We don't try to be Jesus look-alikes on the outside, but instead we are like Jesus on the inside. That means we are kind, loving, and caring. This means there is something inside of us that you can't see, but other people know it's there.

I want people to know I'm a Jesus look-alike, don't you?

Manure Pit

"All of us have become like one who is unclean, and all our righteous acts are like filthy rags" (Isa. 64:6, NIV).

There was a little girl who learned the hard way what the Bible means when it says we have become like one who is unclean.

During the winter in Germany, farmers keep all the farm animals inside the barns, where it is warm. Since there are a lot of cows, horses, pigs, and other animals all living inside the barn, it makes for a big mess. Every day the farmer has to clean the stalls and put down fresh bedding for the animals. Throughout the winter some of the farmers store the manure from the animals in big pits beside their barns. In the spring they pump out the pits into big tanks on wheels called "honey wagons." When the weather warms up, they take their tractors and pull the honey wagon over their fields while spraying the smelly cargo. It really stinks, but it helps make the crops grow.

A long time ago a little German girl named Liesel had a very bad experience with manure pits. She lived in a village where the man who lived next to them had his own little pit by the street.

One day the baker, dressed in his pure white clothes and ringing his bell, came down the street. Liesel and her family came running down the stairs to see what he had on his wagon. Liesel was so excited that she jumped up and down, up and down . . . on the boards covering their neighbor's honey pit!

That's when suddenly Liesel disappeared from sight. Immediately her family heard her screaming from down in the pit. It was awful! She sank in and couldn't get out. Finally, the baker came to her rescue. In his pure white clothes he reached down and pulled her out!

You can guess the rest! Liesel really smelled! Her mama rushed her upstairs and gave her a bath. They even had to throw her clothes away.

We all can learn a lesson from Liesel's terrible experience. That is what it is like to stand alone without Jesus. Without Jesus as our Saviour, God looks upon us as we really are. We stand there dirty, stinking, and in ragged clothes. But Jesus said that if we let Him, He will reach down into the pit and pull us up. He'll clean us up and give us beautiful clothes to wear.

Now, no one in his or her right mind wants to stand around looking and smelling like he or she fell into a manure pit! Jesus simply says that we are to trust Him and He will make us clean. I want one of those beautiful white robes that Jesus gives to His people, don't you? Let Him lift you up today.

Breaking Mom's Favorite Knife

Mischievous Marvin broke his mom's favorite kitchen knife. It wouldn't have been so bad except that his dad had made it just for her. His dad worked in a factory machine shop where he could do special projects in his spare time, so he made Mischievous Marvin's mom a knife with a long shiny blade and hand carved wooden handle. She kept it in a drawer all by itself, and the family called it "the knife," and no one was allowed to use it except Mom.

Well, one day Mischievous Marvin was working outside, building something out of wood. He needed to split the wood in two and couldn't think of a better thing to use than Mom's knife. He slipped into the kitchen and quietly slid the drawer open and got "the knife." Thinking no one would ever know, he sneaked it outside where he was working. In order to split the wood, he held the knife with one hand and hit it with a big hammer. Things were going great. The blade wedged its way through the hard wood and buried itself deeper and deeper.

The going got tougher, however, so Mischievous Marvin pounded harder and harder. Then the worst happened. The knife blade broke in two! It just went plunk, and there it was in two parts. Marvin was in big trouble, and he knew it. There's no such thing as gluing a knife blade back together. Plus, his dad had a very unpleasant method of applying the board of education to Marvin's seat of learning, if you know what I mean. Mischievous Marvin was so shook up that he decided to put the knife back in the drawer while he planned what to do next.

The way he saw it, he had three choices. He could deny he did it. Of course, if the truth came out, it would make bad matters much worse. He could come out and admit he did it, but with conditions. For instance, he could say that the dog made him do it, or maybe the steel in the blade was bad and it would have broken anyway. That didn't seem very convincing either. Finally, he could admit he did it and tell of his sorrow for his disobedience. After all, he *was* really sorry he'd broken his mom's knife. He never planned to break it.

But Mischievous Marvin was a coward. So he left the broken knife in the drawer, and a week or so later he got the punishment he deserved.

In the Bible there is something written for cowardly knife breakers like Mischievous Marvin: *"My dear children, I write this to you so that you will not sin. But if anybody does sin, we have one who speaks to the Father in our defense—Jesus Christ" (1 John 2:1, NIV)*. Furthermore, Jesus said that if we confess our sins He will forgive us of our sins (1 John 1:9).

We have all broken something or done wrong things, am I right? How many of you have broken something? We've all disobeyed and sinned. Isn't it nice to know that Jesus will always forgive us if we admit that we did wrong and are sorry for it? And best of all, Jesus says that He will help us not sin in the future, if we will ask Him. It's like one, two, three. One, ask for forgiveness of your sins. Two, be truly sorry for your sins. And three, ask Jesus to help you not do it again.

A Lesson in a Pear Tree

Gus's friends told him that it was OK, but his conscience told him that it was wrong. But he took his friends' advice and went against his conscience. This turned out to be a bad idea. Here's what happened.

In the fall after school starts in the part of the country where Gus grew up, the pears get ripe. Gus liked pears. In fact, he liked pears a lot. So one day a friend told him about a pear tree he had spotted in a yard across from the school's football field. He said he had tried the pears, and they were really good. Besides, he said, the people didn't care if you picked some.

A day or two later Gus was walking by the football field after school and remembered the pear tree. It had been a long time since lunch, and he was hungry. The thought of a big juicy pear was just too good to pass up.

After some searching, Gus found the tree. It was standing right in the middle of someone's backyard. From where he was standing, he could see that the tree had some really nice pears, but they were up at the top—the easy ones had already been picked. Gus thought it was probably his friend who had gotten those on the lower branches.

Gus stood there and looked at those beautiful pears. His mouth was watering. That's when his conscience reminded him of something he already knew. Taking a pear was *stealing*. But Gus's friends had said the people didn't care. What to do? It didn't look like the people were home, so he couldn't ask for permission. Gus decided to pick just one big pear and go on his way.

The backyard was small, and the pear tree stood right in line with the back door of the house. Feeling a little guilty, Gus climbed way up to the top of the tree and reached out really far to pick a fat juicy pear. That's when the back door opened and out stepped the biggest man Gus had ever seen in his life. The huge man stared at Gus. Thinking to make himself invisible, like some kind of a giant stick bug, Gus froze in place. But Gus noticed the man turn his head, as if he was trying to get a better look at Gus.

Gus must have looked like some strange and unusual pear bear hanging in the top of his tree. The man looked like he really couldn't believe what he was seeing. However, the question of whether Gus was stealing a pear or not became very clear to him as he watched the boy clinging to a high branch in the tree.

It seemed as though a very long time passed. And Gus decided he wasn't hungry anymore. That's when he set a new world's record for leaving a pear tree and racing out of a backyard. Gus was never tempted to return!

The lesson he learned that day was simple: if your conscience says don't do it, then don't do it! Follow what you know is right, and you won't end up full of guilt and fear in a pear tree.

Pigs and People Are Selfish!

"Therefore, if anyone is in Christ, he is a new creation; the old has gone, the new has come!" (2 Cor. 5:17, NIV).

Pigs are selfish; they act just like pigs! Mario found this out first-hand when he helped on his uncle's pig farm in the summer. One of the chores needing to be done early every morning and late in the afternoon was feeding the pigs. Mario's uncle would pull a wagon load of dried corn behind the tractor to the field where the pigs lived. They were kept a long way from the house because they smelled so bad. The pigs (and there were hundreds of them) would run to meet them as they drove in the gate. In the feeding area the pigs, squealing and fighting for a place close to the wagon, would push around under the tractor and the wagon. The pigs were packed so close together that the farmer had to shovel the corn out onto the pigs' backs! They acted just like a herd of selfish pigs!

While Mario's uncle was shoveling out the corn, Mario's job was to take a canoe paddle and stir the slop in a big yellow barrel. It was a mixture of corn and water and other stuff that had soured. It smelled awful, but the pigs loved it. Mario served up the pigs' delight by dipping out bucketfuls and pouring it into long troughs. While serving it, he had to run fast because the pigs would squeal and shove, trying to suck it up as fast as he poured it. Some pigs used to jump right into the trough and lie down so that the other pigs couldn't get any. Mario's uncle finally solved that problem by putting bars across the pig troughs to keep them out.

Mario learned that pigs will be pigs, and that you can't change that. They're born selfish, and they'll die selfish. That's the way pigs are!

People who know pigs say that you can wash a pig and make it all clean and shiny, but the minute you turn your back, it's rolling in the mud again. We know a pig is selfish because it is a pig. It can't help it. It is a pig's character.

But people are different. God made us special. Sometimes boys and girls act like selfish pigs, especially when it comes to sharing and being kind to others. They squeal like pigs, fight, and are selfish. However, people can change. They don't have to act like pigs.

The Bible says that when we accept Jesus into our hearts, He makes us into new creatures. The old is gone, and the new is come. It is done by Jesus. Let pigs be pigs, but let's you and I be like Jesus. Jesus was always kind and willing to share. I want to be like Him, don't you?

Pillar Saints

In the past some people have done some very unusual things to try to please God. A man named Simeon lived on top of a pillar for 36 years. The pillar was like a very tall flagpole with a tiny platform on top. It had a handrail around it so that Simeon wouldn't fall. Simeon remained there for days, weeks, months, and years (36 years, remember) in the driving rain, the bitter cold, and the scorching sun. He was trying to be holy. His followers climbed a ladder to bring him food. Even kings and emperors came to talk to him. People loved him. He died of a leg infection in the year 459, when he was 69 years old.

If we could have talked to Simeon while he was living on his pillar, I think we would have yelled up to him that God loved him just as he was. There was nothing that he could have done to be holy. We would tell him that when Jesus comes into our lives He gives us a new heart. It is not something *we* do, but something *Jesus* does for us.

Simeon was very sincere in what he believed. But does God expect us to spend our lives like Simeon? Based on the fact that Jesus told His disciples to go to all peoples everywhere and make them disciples, we should answer some basic questions.

• If we were to spend our lives living on a pillar, how far could we travel? What about the people in faraway lands? The people would have to come to us, and that's the opposite of what Jesus said to do.

• If we spent our life living on a pillar, how many sick people could we help? How much money would we have to give to the poor and needy?

The point is that doctors, missionaries, nurses, teachers, pastors, police, firefighters, and all the good people who work in other jobs don't live on pillars in the sky. They live and work right down here on the ground with the rest of God's people. Jesus set the example. He walked the dusty roads to tell the people the good news of heaven. Living on a pillar may have been all right for Simeon, but as for me, I'll spend my time down here among the people. What about you?

(See Philip Schaff, *History of the Christian Church*, vol. 3, pp. 191-195.)

Pitcher Plants

"Do not set foot on the path of the wicked or walk in the way of evil men. Avoid it, do not travel on it; turn from it and go on your way" (Prov. 4:14, 15, NIV).

In this case, the only way to go is down. That's what happens to insects that are lured into a sweet-smelling pitcher plant. Pitcher plants look similar to a tall flower vase with a big mouth at the top. They have special leaves that catch rainwater, which makes a small pool inside the plant at the bottom. To attract their next meal, the pitcher plant makes a sweet, sticky nectar that oozes out around the top of the plant, and this lures wasps and other flying insects.

Trying to decide whether to taste the sweet-smelling food, the insects fly around and around the plant. It must smell too good to them, maybe something like freshly baked cookies. Whatever it smells like, once the insects land on the inside of the plant, bad things begin to happen. The insects' feet begin to slowly slide down a slippery slope toward the deadly water below. (The inside of the plant is made like an icy ski slope.) But the nectar tastes so good that the victims don't notice they're getting deeper and deeper into the throat of the plant. The nectar may make the insects drunk, and maybe it even drugs them—scientists aren't sure. (Some scientists think this because the insects can still use their wings to fly and get away, but for some reason they never escape.)

There are temptations similar to that for you and me. Thinking nothing bad will happen to us, we keep circling around trouble time after time. Then one day we decide to do like the insects and taste the nectar. Maybe the nectar will be something that a friend offers to us—something that is supposed to make us high if we sniff it. Maybe someone offers us something to smoke or drink. Whatever it is, we circle around and around the bait until we finally land. That's when our feet start the downhill slide.

Such was the temptation Stephen and Dutch felt when they found the hornets' nest. It was back under a house built on stilts near where the boys lived. The hornets had a nest as big as a pineapple hidden back under the house, where it wasn't bothering anybody.

However, the boys decided to knock it down just for the fun of it. Day after day they threw stones under the house, but they always missed. If a rock hit nearby, the hornets would buzz and threaten, and the boys would run off laughing as the hornets gave up the chase. Day after day they kept coming back and throwing stones, but nothing happened. Then after four days of flirting with trouble, the boys showed up again. Dutch found the perfect rock. It was flat with a sharp edge that fit perfectly into his hand. He pulled back his arm and let the rock fly. A perfect hit! The rock sliced the hornets' nest in two, and the bottom half fell to the ground.

The boys ran, but this time the hornets were deadly serious. Dutch and Stephen ran as fast as they could, but Dutch was faster. The hornets kept coming and caught up with Stephen, the slower runner. Swarming around his head, they took out all their fury. That's the way it is with the devil's temptations. Some of them will sting you really bad, and you'll get over it, like Stephen did, but others can really hurt you! The only safe thing to do is, as the Bible says, *"avoid it, do not travel on it; turn from it and go your way" (Prov. 4:15, NIV).*

Ester on the Pillow

"And the man of God said, Where fell it? And he shewed him the place. And he cut down a stick, and cast it in thither; and the iron did swim. Therefore said he, Take it up to thee. And he put out his hand, and took it" (2 Kings 6:6, 7).

The Kovarsch family worked on a big farm in Germany. One day before Mother left to work in the field, she told her 10-year-old daughter, Heidi, to load up her little sister, Ester, and bring her in the baby carriage out to the field. The mother left on her bicycle, expecting Heidi and her little sister to be along later.

As Mrs. Kovarsch was working, she saw the farm manager riding toward them in a big hurry on his bicycle. He looked worried. When he got to where they were, he told them that their little Ester was not talking and that her mother should rush home. That's all he said.

Mother hopped on her bicycle and rode home as fast as she could. When she hurried into their apartment, she saw little Ester sitting in a big pot of hot water. The little girl screamed for her mother, but everything was OK. However, there was more than met Mother's eye. Here's what happened.

While Mother was working in the field, the two girls had left the house to join her. On the way they had to pass a pond that was surrounded by walnut trees. People were picking up walnuts, and Heidi decided to join in. She left her little sister in the carriage with a pillow on top of her. Everything was just fine, until the carriage started rolling.

It rolled into the pond and sank! But on its way into the water, the carriage turned over and left Baby Ester floating on top of the pillow. The baby was temporarily OK, but no one could swim. The baby floated, the people screamed, but no one could do anything. Finally, a forest ranger's wife came by who could swim. She dived into the icy water and pulled the baby back to safety.

By the time Mother saw the baby, she was being warmed at home in a big pot. Little Ester didn't even get a cold, and her mother still has the pillow!

In 2 Kings 6:6, God, working through the prophet Elisha, performed a miracle and made an axhead swim. This is a case like that one, but this time God made a pillow swim with a baby on it. Whether it was an axhead or a pillow, they were both miracles that God did for one of His children.

Nicked Potatoes

"Offer yourselves as a living sacrifice to God, dedicated to his service and pleasing to him" (Rom. 12:1, TEV).

One fall day the preacher went to visit an old man who had a big garden. The man told the pastor that he had just harvested some beautiful potatoes and that he was proud to be blessed with such a good crop. He asked if the preacher would like to see his prize potatoes. So the pastor, explaining that he also loved potatoes, followed the old man into the dark basement. The preacher said that he loved potatoes so much that he would even eat potato ice cream, if they made it! When the old man turned the basement light on, the preacher was surprised to see so many giant potatoes. If a potato can be beautiful, these were! The whole basement was full of big beauties carefully laid out on newspapers. They were awaiting their final winter storage. His harvest had been truly blessed.

However, a few of his potatoes over in one corner were no longer beautiful. The farmer had injured them when he was digging them up. They would have been perfect except that the shovel used to dig them out had cut places on them. The cuts turned into dark ugly scars. The old man assured the preacher that they were just nicked and that a person could easily cut out the bad spots. Laying out some of the injured ones on a paper, the old farmer smiled and told the preacher to take them with him as a gift from his garden. The pastor wrapped up the little pile of bad potatoes in a newspaper and felt sorry for the old man. His gift was a selfish gift. You see, the farmer really didn't want to share, but he felt he had to do something, so he gave the preacher his rejects to make himself feel good.

The Bible says that we are to give ourselves as an offering to God. That means giving our lives in service for Jesus. We are to give the best we have in service to Him. Whether we grow up to be janitors, barbers, factory workers, doctors, lawyers, teachers, preachers, or whatever, we are to be the best we can be for God. The reason why we give God our best is that He gave His best to us when He sent Jesus to this earth to save us. The Bible says: *"For God loved the world so much that he gave his only Son, so that everyone who believes in him may not die but have eternal life. For God did not send his Son into the world to be its judge, but to be its savior" (John 3:16, 17, TEV).*

Shouldn't we always remember to give back our best to Him? Will you agree with me that whatever we do, we'll always give our best in thanks to God for what He has done for us? *"Honor the Lord by making him an offering from the best of all that your land produces" (Prov. 3:9, TEV).*

Your Smoke Will Find You Out!

Firebug Fred was a slow learner about the danger of playing with matches and fire. He loved to make campfires in the yard. One of his early experiments was a stove made out of a cement block stuffed full of sticks. It produced a little fire that Fred used to cook coffee grounds and water in a soup can—like something he saw the cowboys do in the movies. That didn't work so well, and the brew tasted terrible. Of course, his stove was built in secret, since his dad had forbidden him to make fires.

Firebug Fred wasn't a real firebug or anything like that. He just liked to build little campfires. His main problem was that he was too young to understand the dangers of fire. Since his mom and dad had forbidden him to build any more fires, he gave up for a while. Until . . .

One day Mother and Father left Fred alone while they went to visit friends. Firebug Fred doesn't know how or why, but he decided to build a small campfire where they would never find him out. So he thought and thought. It had to be small, and surely it couldn't be outside where they would see it, so he built the fire in their closet! That's right! He pushed their clothes out of the way and built a little fire right there in the clothes closet! Like I said, Firebug Fred was a slow learner.

Well, the fire started out small, it was just a teeny weeny one. But then, unexpectedly—at least to Fred—the flames really flared up when he put the paper on the fire, and then he got scared. Firebug Fred rushed into action, and before the fire got out of hand, he was able to smother it and clean up the mess. It left only a little scorch mark on the floor. Fred reasoned that everything was all right and that he'd never be found out. So he went on his way, not thinking about the smoky odor left in his parents' clothes.

It was the next day before his smoke found him out. We'll leave out the painful details of what exactly happened to Firebug Fred. But I will tell you this—he couldn't sit very well for some time.

Today when he looks back, he asks himself how he could have done something so stupid. However, the Bible says we have all sinned and come short of the glory of God. It goes on to say: *"Happy are those whose wrongs are forgiven, whose sins are pardoned! Happy is the person whose sins the Lord will not keep account of!" (Rom. 4:7, 8, TEV).*

Jesus told us that He will forgive our sins if we will confess them. Even slow learners who set fires in closets can be forgiven—and so can you. Won't you ask Him today to forgive your sins and wash away that old smoky odor and clean up your heart?

The Little Purse
With the Blue Flowers

Aunt Ella had a little white leather bag about the size of your hand. It had a drawstring around the top, and it was decorated with a circle of pretty little blue flowers. Her niece Heidi used to love to play with it. It was just the right size for a little girl. And Heidi would imagine that it was filled with diamonds, pearls, gold jewelry, or whatever little girls would put in such a lovely little bag.

Every time Heidi went to visit her aunt, she would ask to play with the little white bag. How she loved to pretend that it was hers! She wanted it badly, but was always told to put it back on the shelf when she had to go, and that she could play with it the next time she came to visit. Aunt Ella felt that Heidi wasn't quite old enough to take care of it, because it was very expensive.

Then one day while visiting her aunt, Heidi was asked to stay with her cousin Jergen while Aunt Ella went shopping. Heidi knew that her aunt didn't use the purse and didn't really need it . . . so she stole it. She took it home and hid it. Now and then she would get it out and secretly play with the little purse, but she had to keep it out of sight so that the rest of the family wouldn't see it.

Then came the day Heidi was dreading. Aunt Ella asked her if she had seen the bag. Heidi lied and said she didn't know anything about it. Her aunt looked disappointed and told Heidi that she knew how much Heidi loved the bag, so she'd been hunting for it so that she could give it to her.

Now Heidi had a real big problem. She had the bag, but could only play with it in secret. To make matters worse, she was a liar who was ashamed of what she had done. What to do? Well, Heidi secretly put the bag back. Then a little later her aunt pretended to find it. Aunt Ella had actually known all along where the bag was, but she was a nice lady and wanted to do what was best for Heidi.

After some time had passed, she presented the bag to Heidi, and they both pretended to be surprised. Heidi vowed from that day forward never to steal again. It wasn't worth it. It never is!

Raindrops and Mustard Seeds

"The kingdom of heaven is like to a grain of mustard seed, which a man took, and sowed in his field: Which indeed is the least of all seeds: but when it is grown, it is the greatest among herbs, and becometh a tree, so that the birds of the air come and lodge in the branches thereof" (Matt. 13:31, 32).

Every raindrop has a little bit of dust in it. When a raindrop dries, it leaves a tiny bit of dust behind. I'm sure you've seen rain spots on your windows at home or on the windshield of a car. Maybe you've even helped wash them off. However, that same little bit of dust can be like a seed planted way up in the sky. I say this because raindrops will not form unless they have that little speck to help them start.

Now, once a raindrop forms, it can either become good or bad, depending on how things are up there where it is formed. If the air is warm, the little drop grows until it is big enough to fall out of the sky and onto some thirsty plant on the earth to give it a welcome drink. If the air is cold and still, and everything is just right, the little drops turn into snowflakes, which cover the ground with a beautiful white blanket.

However, if the air is cold and blowing, some very bad things can happen to the little raindrop. As it falls through the sky, it can freeze into a little ball of ice. Then if the wind blows straight up, as it sometimes does, the little ball of ice is carried back up and picks up some more water. It gets heavier and falls toward the earth again and freezes into a larger ice ball. But if the wind blows straight up again, the ball of ice travels back up and picks up still more water. This can happen again and again, until these balls of ice—or hailstones—get as big as baseballs.

Finally the hailstones get so heavy that the wind can't blow them back up anymore, and they fall to earth. We call that a hailstorm. If it happens during the summer growing season, it can cut the leaves off the plants and destroy lots of crops. Hailstones also damage houses and cars, and do much other harm.

However, we should remember that raindrops and the hailstones all start from the same place. It is what happens to them before they reach the earth that makes the difference. One is good; one is bad. Jesus said that we Christians need just a tiny bit of faith—as small as a mustard seed—to do great things for God. If we ask Him, He will give us the seed of faith that we need to become a raindrop for Him.

Of course, a raindrop does not have a choice as to what it will become, but we do. I want to be a raindrop for Jesus. Don't you?

Shooting Out the Railroad Signal Lights

There was a man who fixed railroad signal lights, and he had an interesting story to tell. He worked on all the signal lights along the tracks, and also the red lights you see flashing at railroad crossings when a train is coming.

One day he was called to repair one of those big signal lights that are on towers beside the tracks. They have green, yellow, and red lights and are like traffic lights for trains. When he got there he found that the bulbs had been shot out with a rifle, so he called the railroad detective to investigate.

The investigator found on the ground a number of empty rifle shells from a gun about the size a boy might own. He thought that a kid from the neighborhood probably used the lights for target practice. So he told the repairman he would check the area for the next few days and see if the boy would return. And sure enough, the very next day the boy was back. The detective caught him with his .22 caliber rifle. He was shooting at things around the tracks. Saying how sorry he was, the young man admitted to the crime and hung his head in shame. The detective told him how dangerous it is if the lights don't work, and the boy promised never to do it again.

Even though the detective felt that the boy was truly sorry, he still wanted to talk to the boy's parents. So he asked the boy where he lived. The boy told the detective that his house was just up the road. He pointed to a little white house in the distance and then said his parents would not be home until 7:00 p.m. The detective took the boy's name and told him he would be back that evening to see his parents.

It was after dark when the detective went to the little house. He knocked and knocked on the door. After a long time an old man and his wife came to the door. They didn't know the little boy or anyone who looked like him. The boy had lied. So the next day the railroad detective went to school and asked if the teachers knew the boy. They didn't know him either. You see, he had also lied about his name. You can guess what happened when the detective visited the neighbors around where the boy was shooting. They had never heard of the fellow either. The boy was a very skilled liar. He had totally fooled the detective and escaped without punishment . . . or had he?

The question is this: Who got hurt the most because of the boy's lie? He did! He could never return to the neighborhood because he knew that everyone was looking for him. One wonders how many times he had to run and hide when he was outside playing because he thought he saw the detective coming. And even today, although he is grown up, he must wonder if the detective would still recognize him.

When we lie, who gets hurt the most? We do! God, speaking through the apostle Paul, said: *"Do not lie to one another, for you have put off the old self with its habits and have put on the new self"* *(Col. 3:9, 10, TEV).* Christian boys and girls have been made into new people because they have Jesus in their hearts. Therefore, Jesus wants us not to lie to each other for our own good. That way we won't have to go around worrying like the boy who shot out the railroad lights still does.

The Seeds Will Come Up!

A long time ago in South Carolina, in 1922 to be exact, a boy named G. S. Cain lived on a little farm. Back then they grew almost everything they ate right there on the family farm. If they went to town, it was to trade some of their crops for salt, sugar, and maybe some candy for the children. The children worked right alongside their mom and dad out in the fields. In July of that long ago year, it came time to plant the peas for the family to eat during the next winter. In July they planted their peas between the rows in the cornfield so that the pea vines could climb up the corn stalks and be ready for picking in October.

Little G. S. Cain was given the job of planting the peas. His father told him to walk ahead of the horse as it pulled the plow through the corn. The idea was that G. S. Cain would drop a pinch of peas at every step. This would make a little hill of about six or eight peas in the dirt, and the plow would cover them up when the horse came along.

Everything went along OK for about eight or 10 rows. Then G. S. Cain began to get hot. The bucketful of peas began to get heavy. Since it was July and G. S. Cain was only 12 years old, the tops of the corn were over his head and blocking the summer breeze. He got so hot that he thought he'd take a short break under a tree at the edge of the field. He was way ahead of the horse and plow, so he had some extra time to loaf. It was then and there, as he was lying under that tree in the cool shade, that he dreamed up a scheme that got him into big trouble.

Going back into the corn after his rest, he carried out his plan. He dug out a hole in the soft dirt with his feet and buried the remaining two gallons of peas right there between the rows of corn! Although his dad was surprised at how fast he'd gotten the job done, G. S. Cain was sure he had gotten away with his little scheme. Everything was just fine . . . until a week later when it rained. That July rain was very welcome to the thirsty peas. Three days later they did what planted peas do. They came up. And G. S. Cain's daddy went out to inspect the field. As he walked the first eight rows, everything seemed just fine, but then he came upon an area that he described as having peas growing thicker than hair on a dog's back.

You can guess the rest. When Mr. Cain got back from the field, he talked very seriously with his son and quoted Galatians 6:7: *"A man reaps what he sows" (NIV).*

G. S. Cain learned a hard lesson about obedience. If his daddy had not discovered what had been done, the whole family would have had less to eat during the cold winter months. The whole family would have suffered because of one lazy little boy.

Jesus asks for each of us to be obedient and do what He asks— and for a good reason. It's good for us. If we do what we know is right, and love and serve Jesus with all our hearts, we will never have to worry about those hidden seeds coming up.

He Killed the Red Rooster

"And be sure your sin will find you out" (Num. 32:23).

Jerry and his cousin Randall loved to throw rocks. They threw at trees; they threw at buildings; and they threw stones at anything that moved. But they never hit anything. The 10-year-old cousins couldn't hit the broad side of a barn. However, because of his rock throwing, Jerry would soon learn firsthand what a Bible text means that says your sin will find you out.

It started one day when they went to visit their grandma and grandpa on the farm. Grandma had warned them kindly, "Boys, don't throw rocks here. You could break out a window or maybe even hurt someone." Of course, after Grandma went back in the house, it wasn't long until Jerry and Randall slipped out of sight and returned to their old habit of throwing rocks.

It was about this time that the old rooster decided to take a stroll across the barnyard. He was a big red rooster called a dominique. He had a black face, shiny eyes, a red rose comb on top of his head, a bright yellow beak, and red ear lobes. Grandma called him the "yard bird" because he was the granddaddy and boss of all the chickens in the barnyard.

The old red rooster was taking his good old time and doing what big roosters do. He'd take a few steps and then scratch the dirt with his big yellow feet and eat a bug or two. Next he'd chase a few of the younger chickens in circles and then proudly raise up on his toes and crow.

That's when Jerry noticed that the old rooster had his back turned and Jerry just happened to have a rock in his hand. If he tried real hard, Jerry wondered, could he hit the old rooster? So he pulled his arm back, and with all his might he let the stone fly.

Clunk! was the sound that the rock made when it hit the old rooster squarely in the back of the head. Jerry turned to Randall, his eyes as big as saucers. He couldn't believe it he actually hit the rooster!

The boys ran up to the old red rooster to see what the rock had done, but the rooster didn't move. He just lay there on the ground, with the rock beside him. Jerry panicked. "I killed the rooster, I killed the rooster!" He didn't know what to do. He felt ashamed, afraid, and downright scared. What would happen once Grandma found out what happened to her pet rooster? So the two boys decided to take the rooster and throw him in the briar patch out behind Grandpa's barn. They tossed him back behind the bushes and then ran off to play just as if nothing ever happened.

But that night Jerry had a problem with his conscience. It kept reminding him of his sin. All night long he tossed and turned as he tried to decide what to do. He knew it was wrong to have thrown the rock and he also knew it was even worse to hide what he'd done.

The next morning he couldn't take it anymore and confessed to his grandma. He explained that he'd thrown the stone and that he was sorry for hiding the rooster behind the barn.

But Grandma did the strangest thing, she laughed. She broke out laughing and then got serious again. Real serious like, she turned to Jerry and said, "You didn't kill that old rooster. I saw him walking around the yard this morning."

Jerry was so relieved, he wanted to shout for joy.

Of course, there still was the problem of Jerry's disobedience. Grandpa handled that in such a way that Jerry always thought before he threw stones again.

The Dog That Laughed
All the Way Home

"There are different abilities to perform service, but the same God gives ability to everyone for their particular service" (1 Cor. 12:6, TEV).

Wayne came home one day and heard the neighbor lady calling for him to come over to her house immediately. When Wayne got there, he saw his little beagle dog lying on the ground and flopping around like a fish out of the water. The dog was foaming at the mouth and acting crazy with a weird look in its eyes.

Wayne carefully picked up his dog and took it home, all the while thinking the worst—that his little dog had rabies. He put the dog in a horse trailer with high side rails that would keep the dog from escaping. Then he ran into the house and called the veterinarian. Hurriedly he explained all about the strange way his dog was acting. Sadly, he found out that the only way to tell for sure if his dog had rabies was to analyze its brain cells. Of course, this meant the death of his little beagle.

Wayne hung up the phone after agreeing to take his dog to the veterinarian. It looked very bad for his little pet. After making up his mind about what he had to do, he went outside to get the dog out of the trailer. When he walked up, the little beagle saw him coming and got so excited that it jumped clear over the top of the trailer and landed on Wayne's face. As the dog struggled to keep from falling, it scratched Wayne's face and got some foam from its mouth into the bleeding scratches. This was really bad, because it looked as if the dog had just given Wayne rabies.

Wayne, scared and upset for his dog and for himself, tied a rope around its neck and put it in the front of his pickup truck. As Wayne drove to the veterinarian, the dog kept acting crazy, biting the seat, attacking the gear shift, and foaming at the mouth. Wayne fought the dog all the way to the animal doctor. When he drove up, the veterinarian immediately came outside, and Wayne pulled his wild dog from the truck. The veterinarian took one look and said, "Bring him inside. He's got a bone in his throat."

Wayne was astonished. He thought for sure the doctor would shoot his dog right there in the parking lot. Instead, the veterinarian simply took his fingers and forced the dog's mouth open, reached down its throat, and popped out a bone! It was just a little bone. A bone about two inches long and as big around as a pencil.

Wayne said that if a dog could sigh with relief, his beagle did. It immediately calmed down, stopped foaming at the mouth, and began to smile almost like a human. On the way home, the dog sat up on the seat just like he was a little king enjoying the scenery passing by.

Thanks to his training, the veterinarian knew just what to do. He saved the dog's life. But we should remember that God gave the veterinarian the gift of helping animals. Surely the man went to school and learned all he could about animals, but God gave him the ability and the gift to become an animal doctor.

God gives each of us gifts. Some of you might indeed grow up to be veterinarians; others of you may be people doctors, or teachers, or preachers, or nurses, or police officers. Whatever gift God gives us, it is up to us to learn all we can and then use it to help others. Aren't you glad God gave us all different and special gifts to help each other? I wonder what gift He gave you? What will you do with it?

Soft Spots

"Put on all the armor that God gives you, so that you will be able to stand up against the Devil's evil tricks" (Eph. 6:11, TEV).

The armadillo and the porcupine have armor to protect themselves. When the armadillo is attacked, it rolls up into an armor-plated ball that few animals can get a grip on. If a porcupine is attacked, it humps up its back and forms a big ball of quills. Both animals are protecting their bellies, their soft spots, where another animal could hurt them.

Some very big animals also have some very soft spots. Frank proved that down at his neighbor's dairy farm. It was spring, and all the neighborhood kids bought squirt guns. These were just little things that you could carry in your pocket. They were not the mega-assault water cannons that you see today. Well anyway, one evening Frank and a friend were helping bring in the cows for milking. They were playing along the way and shooting each other with their water pistols, and occasionally a cow or two in the backside. When they got into the barn lot, the two boys walked ahead of the cows, and that's when Frank turned around and shot one of them in the nose. The squirt of water on the cow's soft nose so shocked her that she dropped down onto one knee.

Frank turned to see the farmer running up and asking what he had done. Frank thought the farmer was angry, but instead he wanted him to try to do it again. Frank squirted once more, but the cow only looked at him like he wasn't too smart to try the same trick the second time, and she went on her way. Frank made his point—cows definitely have soft spots on their noses, and as he learned later, so do pigs.

If you go to a county fair, you're likely to see people leading their pigs around by the nose. Farmers have a long stick with a pair of fingers on the end that they clamp into the pig's nose holes. It doesn't hurt as long as the pig follows along quietly. Pigs, cows, and animals of all sorts have their soft spots, and so do you and I!

Sometimes boys' and girls' biggest soft spots are the things other people call them. No one likes to be called a chicken or a wimp. But our friends know if they call us one of these names, they're touching our soft spot. Have you ever had someone dare you to do something? Sure you have, and probably some of the times you were dared, you did what they asked just to show them you were not afraid. Often people try to talk us into doing things that we know are wrong. They touch our soft spot and tell us that doing something wrong will be all right if we only do it once. They may even try to get us to take drugs or some other gross thing. But Solomon said: *"Those who plan evil are in for a rude surprise, but those who work for good will find happiness"* (Prov. 12:20, TEV).

Because of our soft spots, God tells us to put on the armor that He gives, and we will always have His protection.

The Little Things Make a Difference

Steve's dad bought an old swimming pool from a friend. Since it was used, there were no instructions about how to put it together. It was one of those above-ground types, with a platform around the sides.

For weeks Steve helped his dad work, finding and fitting all the pieces together as best they could. It was like a big puzzle. *After all,* his dad thought, *anyone can put a swimming pool together.* He bolted all the pieces in place and filled it to the top with water. But no swimmers were allowed in until all the family could be there for the first swimming party.

Finally the day came. A picnic table for lunch was set out by the pool. It was loaded down with good food—homemade potato salad, Grandma's macaroni and cheese casserole, and Aunt Pat's special super-duper cake.

The older folk sat around the table, while a crowd of Steve's cousins pushed and shoved at poolside. Finally the moment arrived. Everyone watched as the signal was given and the kids all dived into the pool at once.

What happened next is not entirely clear. It was not good, however. We do know there was a loud boom as the pool's seam broke open from the top to the bottom!

Steve's little sister screamed, "Hit it!" and ran off like a deer. The old folks just sat and stared. They said it looked like an ocean wave coming. That day the potato salad went surfing, and the macaroni casserole balanced on the top of the wave. Grandma, a nonswimmer, was sucked into the wave and began tumbling feet over head in the grass.

After the flood had passed, she said, "I was thinking, *I can't swim! I'm going to drown right here in the backyard!*" But she grabbed onto the neighbor's hedge and rode out the flood safely.

As the wave flowed on, it made a giant splash against the house and washed the petunias right out of their flower beds. Then everything got quiet. All that was left behind was Steve and a bunch of kids standing in an empty pool and looking at a yard covered with potato salad, macaroni, and wet adults. No one was hurt, so they cleaned up the mess and went home.

Steve and his dad went back to work. This time they talked to someone who knew what to do, and they succeeded in putting the pool back together correctly. Steve's dad found that he had left some very important parts out the first time he put the pool together—two small steel bars that held the seam tight. Several days later they had another swimming party, but this time the pool didn't burst.

Steve and his daddy learned something very important. Pay attention to the little things, and the big things will take care of themselves.

For you and me who do not have swimming pools to put together, taking care of the little things means studying and praying every day. It means being kind and honest, and sharing with other kids. It means that Jesus will take care of the bigger things and we are to take care of the little things He asks us to do.

What's the Difference?

"Honor your father and your mother" (Ex. 20:12, NIV).

[This exercise takes the young people through increasing degrees of difficulty, until they are asked how to define right from wrong. It is intended to be used as a friendly question-and-answer session.]

I. Apples and Oranges (These are easy to tell the difference.)

    A. Apples

        1. Skin texture (smooth skin)

        2. Color (usually red, but can be green or yellow)

        3. Taste

    B. Oranges

        1. Skin texture (leathery, not smooth skin)

        2. Color (usually orange)

        3. Taste

    C. The Major Difference: The taste

II. Lemons and Limes (These are harder to tell the difference.)

    A. Lemons

        1. Skin texture (like an orange)

        2. Color (yellow)

        3. Taste

    B. Limes

        1. Skin texture (like a lemon)

        2. Color (green)

        3. Taste

    C. The Major Difference: The color

III. Oranges and Tangerines (These are even harder to tell the difference.)

    A. Oranges

        1. Skin texture (leathery, covered with tiny bumps)

2. Color (usually orange)

3. Taste

B. Tangerines

  1. Skin texture (leathery, almost like an orange)

  2. Color (reddish orange)

  3. Taste

C. The Major Difference: The taste

IV. Toadstools and Mushrooms (Very hard to tell the difference.)

A. Toadstools

  1. Skin texture (just like the mushroom's)

  2. Color (just like the mushroom's)

B. Mushrooms

  1. Skin texture (just like the toadstool's)

  2. Color (just like the toadstool's)

C. The Major Difference:

1. There are more than 3,000 different kinds of mushrooms and toadstools. Some will kill you, and others are good to eat. Generally the name "mushroom" is given to the kinds that can be eaten. Those that are poisonous are called "toadstools." Botanists put them all in the same group.

2. If you find plants that look like mushrooms in the woods, you should never eat them. Only experts can tell which will kill you and which won't.

V. Right and Wrong

Sometimes right and wrong look very much the same, just like toadstools and mushrooms. It is very hard to tell the difference. How can you know the difference between right and wrong, good and bad?

1. Listen to your parents.

2. Listen to your teachers.

3. Study for yourself, and let the Holy Spirit impress you as to what is right and wrong.

4. Pray for Jesus to guide you to always do right.

5. Never violate your conscience. If you feel like it is wrong, don't do it.

Concluding Thought: Without Jesus it is sometimes very hard to tell the difference between right and wrong. Listen to Him speak through your parents or guardians, and then do what is right. As it says in the Ten Commandments: *"Respect your father and your mother" (Ex. 20:12, TEV).*

Shotgun Blast

"If we confess our sins, he is faithful and just and will forgive us our sins and purify us from all unrighteousness" *(1 John 1:9, NIV).*

Todd and Tom had been deer hunting in a nearby woods. Todd had a .12 gauge, double-barrel shotgun that he unloaded before he and Tom came into the house that afternoon. It was during the Christmas holidays, and Todd's house was full of guests. The boys were planning to go to Todd's room and hang out there for a while and then go hunting again.

As they were walking down the hall to his bedroom, Todd's dad called out to him. The three of them stood in the hallway as they talked about what the boys had seen and about going out hunting again a little later in the day. While Todd talked to his dad, he rested his gun barrel on his toe and played with the triggers. When their conversation ended, Todd pointed the gun barrel down into the carpet and tickled the trigger one too many times.

Bam! The shotgun went off, blasting a hole through the floor and blowing a small crater in the dirt under the house! Smelly gun smoke filled the house, and everyone's ears rang from the gun blast. Todd stood there shaking in unbelief as his father frantically looked to see if his son still had his toes. Todd jumped back and exclaimed, "It wasn't loaded! It wasn't loaded, was it Tom?"

No one was hurt. Everyone was OK, that is, except for being frightened out of their skins and upset with Todd. Finally, Todd stopped denying the obvious and admitted that the gun must have been loaded. From that point forward, things took a turn for the better. Once Todd admitted that he had done wrong, he was able to ask for forgiveness. Then after his family calmed down, they forgave him and patched the hole in the floor.

Jesus tells us that if we will confess our sins, He is faithful and true to forgive us of our sins. Of course, we have to first realize that we are sinners and then ask for forgiveness. But there is one thing that Jesus can't do. He can't go back and patch the holes that we have made in our lives. Someone has said that sin is like a nail in a board. You can ask Jesus to forgive you of the sin, but when He pulls out the nail, the nail hole is still there.

But when we get to heaven, Jesus will also remove the holes. If we ask Him to forgive us of our sins, He will eventually make us all brand new! The Bible says: *"My dear children, I write this to you so that you will not sin. But if anybody does sin, we have one who speaks to the Father in our defense—Jesus Christ, the Righteous One" (1 John 2:1, NIV).* Aren't you thankful that there will be no bullet holes in heaven?

By the way, Todd and Tom never did shoot a deer and probably never will!

Trust Your Conscience

"Children, obey your parents in all things: for this is well pleasing unto the Lord" (Col. 3:20).

If an animal moves, it has to know which way is up, and it has to stay in balance! So do you. We've all had somebody spin us around and around, and then when we try to walk, we stumble around and fall down. It's because we have confused the little part in our ear that keeps us in balance.

Other living things that move also have little parts to keep them walking or moving upright. Whether they be fish in the lake, birds in the air, or jellyfish in the sea, they all have special parts to keep them balanced.

However, for humans, whom God created with the ability to think on their own, there is something special that no other creature has—the conscience. This little story will help me explain.

Steve and his brother, Dortch, wanted to go fishing at a lake that was not far from their house. Neither of them could swim, so their mother told them she just didn't feel right allowing them to go fishing alone. The boys fussed about Mom not being fair and then went outside to play.

However, it wasn't long until one of them figured out that Mom would never know if they quietly slipped down the hill, where she couldn't see them, and went fishing anyway. They decided to dig a few worms, sneak off to the lake, and be back before she even noticed they were gone. It sounded like a foolproof plan, but they made three big mistakes that afternoon.

Quietly taking their fishing poles and a shovel to dig some worms, they sneaked down the hill. That was their first mistake. Out of Mom's sight, they began digging for worms in what seemed to be a nice soft spot. The digging was easy. That was their second mistake! They found out that the spot was soft because they were digging up a nest of yellow jackets! As the angry wasps stung the boys, they ran up the hill to get away. That was their third and final mistake. You don't try to get away from furious wasps by running uphill. Everyone knows if you want to run fast, you should run downhill!

Needless to say, Steve and Dortch didn't go fishing.

However, all this would never have happened if they had only followed their consciences. I mean, if they had to sneak away, they already knew that what they were doing was wrong. Their consciences had already told them, "Don't do it." That's the way the conscience works. God has put within us a part that keeps us in balance. It keeps us from falling into difficulty and getting hurt. When we want to do something wrong, our consciences tell us, "Don't do it, or you'll get yourself in trouble."

There are three lessons here that you should never forget about how your conscience keeps you in balance. The first is that you should never, never do something against what your conscience tells you. Second, you should always obey your parents or guardians. And finally, never try to outrun a swarm of wasps by running uphill!

PART III

OBJECT LESSONS

The Anglerfish

"Be alert, be on watch! Your enemy, the Devil, roams around like a roaring lion, looking for someone to devour" (1 Peter 5:8, TEV).

Visual Aid: A bag of cookies tied to a fishing pole.

Did you know there's a fish that fishes for fish? This fish likes to devour other fish, which means it eats them up. It's called the anglerfish. The anglerfish hides on the bottom of the ocean and waits for a smaller fish to swim by. When it sees one coming, it raises on top of its head a little flagpole with a piece of make-believe bait on it and waves it back and forth.

The anglerfish keeps waving it around until it finally catches the attention of an innocent little fish passing by. The bait looks very tempting as it wriggles back and forth. Can't you imagine what it must be like? Maybe the little fish thinks it sees something like a giant fish cookie floating in front. Finally, the little fish's curiosity gets the best of it, and it swims up closer for a better look. That is *not* a good idea!

Can't you just imagine the little fish blinking its eyes and shaking its head . . . not believing what it's seeing? *Can this really be a giant fish cookie?* Then when the little fish is just where the anglerfish wants it, the anglerfish throws open its mouth, and the little fish is washed in a rushing stream into the jaws of the big fish. There is no escape. The little fish becomes the cookie, as the big fish licks its lips and begins wiggling its flagpole again.

Of course, the anglerfish's bait is not real food. It's just a little piece of skin that looks like something it is not. It may not even look real, but it serves its deadly purpose. That is, it catches the attention of the little fish just long enough for the big fish to make its move. That is the fatal mistake that little fish often make. They keep their

125

eyes on the bait instead of on the giant fish that's waving it.

A text in the Bible says: *"Be alert, be on watch! Your enemy, the Devil, roams around like a roaring lion, looking for someone to devour" (1 Peter 5:8, TEV).* In a way he's a lot like the anglerfish. The devil has things to offer you that are not always what they may seem. The devil may wave something around in your face that looks like a lot of fun . . . but it's just the devil's bait. If someone wants to give you some drugs to try, they are really offering you the devil's bait. It may sound like fun to try something new. You may be told that it won't hurt to try it just once. That's when you need to remember the anglerfish and how it gets its next meal.

Remember, the little fish only stopped once to see what was going on. The next thing it knew, it was in the belly of the big fish. So don't forget: if you take the bait, the devil is just waiting to swallow you whole!

Don't be like the little fish that the anglerfish had for supper. Get your eye off the bait and look at who is behind the offer! If it's drugs, you can be sure the devil is behind it, and he is seeking to devour you whole!

Object Lesson 2

Bound Together

Visual Aid: A large book. (I use an expensive looking hard-cover book that I purchased for a dollar at a flea market.)

"[The Lord] does not want anyone to be destroyed, but wants all to turn away from their sins" (2 Peter 3:9, TEV).

You are very important to Jesus and to His church. I've brought this book along to show you what I mean. You all know that a book is made up of pages all stuck together with glue along one edge. We call that the spine.

[Show the book; open it up and point out the spine.]

When people write books, they divide up the material into chapters. For instance, if I were writing a book about churches, I would make chapters about the First Street church, the Second Street church, the Third Street church, and so on. Every church would have its own separate chapter.

[Show how your book is divided into chapters.]

The next thing about books is that a chapter may have a lot of pages or sometimes just a few. In the case of my example about churches, every church member would be a page of a chapter. There would be a page for Mr. Smith, another page for Mrs. Smith, still another for Billy Smith, yet another for Betty Smith, and a page for each member of the Jones family also. Every church member would have his or her own special page, because every member is important to Jesus.

[Hold the book up and make the following point about strength in unity.]

So just how important are you? You are *very* important, because when everyone is together, the church is strong. Let me demonstrate what I mean. Is there anyone here who thinks he or she is really strong?

[Choose a child and ask him or her to tear the entire book in two. Obviously the attempt will be fruitless. However, to underscore the point, ask the same child to reach into the book and tear out a single page. The child will be reluctant to tear up a book, so this would be a good time to explain that this is not really a valuable book.

[Once the child has torn out the sheet, have another child tear the sheet into pieces. The point is obvious. When a page is removed from the book, the page is weak and easily destroyed.]

The Bible says: *"How wonderful it is, how pleasant, for God's people to live together in harmony!" (Ps. 133:1, TEV).*

Boys and girls, when we attend church every week, as we should, and when we live our lives as loving Christians, we help make God's church strong. When we all work together and stay close together like pages glued into a book, then the Lord's church is strong.

Don't forget! You may be just one little page in God's book, but when you're missing, you can make a big difference.

OR

Don't forget! Your strength is being a part of God's book. People who tear themselves out of the book are like a single page all by itself.

On God's Time

Visual Aid: A flower in full bloom along with some buds almost ready to open. [A rose or amaryllis works well.]

I enjoy flowers. I like the way they look and the way *most* of them smell! In the spring, after the cold days of winter, I enjoy watching the flowers pop through the warm soil, grow up tall, put on buds, and then burst into blossoms in the warm sunshine. Sometimes I feel that I just can't wait to see the flower buds unfold. Maybe some of you have also felt like that. You want to take the bud and help it unfold before its time. Anyone ever tried that?

Today I've brought along this [amaryllis] plant that has this beautiful [trumpet shaped] flower and some buds that haven't opened up yet. I wonder if one of you would open a bud for us so that we can see how pretty the flower is that's still inside?

[At this point have a child volunteer to peel one of the buds open. Naturally the frustrated child destroys the bud.]

I guess the bud wasn't ready to open up yet. It wasn't time. Do you think maybe we should have waited until the bud opened on its own? I think we've learned that it's like the Bible says: "Everything that happens in this world happens at the time God chooses" (Eccl. 3:1, TEV). Jesus said: *"First the tender stalk appears, then the head, and finally the head full of grain" (Mark 4:28, TEV).* It all takes time. That's the way God planned it. And that's the way it is with boys and girls.

As we grow up we start out as little plants that take a long time and a lot of patience to become a full blooming flower in God's garden. Part of that growing up is going to school and then on to college. Another part is coming to church and learning about Jesus. As we grow and learn, we change from buds to flowers for God.

However, if we quit growing along the way, we never blossom into all that God wants us to be. If you get impatient and wish you could hurry up and grow up, remember that God is not finished with you yet. When the time is right, He will make you a beautiful flower in His garden.

The Bull and Chain

Visual Aid: A heavy rope with a snap on the end.

When City Boy Roy was growing up in Ohio, he used to visit his grandpa's farm. For a while Grandfather kept a huge bull on his farm. Of course, you know that a bull is a male cow. This one was almost the size of a buffalo, and it had big horns and a bad temper. Bulls are big, but not very smart. A dog will come when you call its name, but a bull won't. He's just not bright enough to understand that his name is being called.

City Boy Roy's grandpa's bull liked to escape and go visit the neighbor's cows. That bull was so strong that he could easily break down any fence in the pasture and run off any time he wanted. Roy's grandpa got tired of rounding up his runaway bull. It seemed like every time Grandpa let the bull out in the field to graze, that big old animal would run off to visit the girl cows at the neighbor's farm. He never learned to stay home. So most of the time Grandpa kept the bull locked in a corral called the bull pen, next to the barn.

Because of his bad temper the bull was dangerous. So when City Boy Roy went to visit Grandpa, Roy would always check to see if the bull was out. If he was in the pasture grazing, Roy didn't go near him. But City Boy Roy's grandpa wasn't afraid of the bull. Even though Grandpa was only an average-sized man, he could lead that giant bull around without any fear. How? It was simple.

You see, a bull's nose is very tender, so Grandpa put a big brass ring right through the soft area between the big bull's nostrils. You can imagine how it would hurt if someone pulled on the ring. And that's exactly what Roy's grandpa did. He hooked a chain through the ring and pulled on it when he wanted the bull to follow him.

Leading the bull around by the nose was easy. It simply hurt too much for the bull *not* to do what Grandpa wanted. Of course, you must remember that the chain in the ring did not hurt the bull if he obeyed. What a sight to see City Boy Roy's grandpa leading around an animal that stood taller than he and weighed as much as a small car! The bull always came along obediently as long as Roy's grandpa held the chain.

When I think of that bull with the chain in his nose, I think of what happens to us when we sin. If we lie, cheat, steal, or do some other gross sin, the devil puts a ring of sin through our nose and leads us around. He makes slaves out of us. But the Bible tells us that Jesus came to set the captives free. He came to remove the ring and chain from our noses.

Trusting in Him, we follow Jesus because we *want* to, not because we *have* to.

Making Corn Bread or Cake

Visual Aids: All of the ingredients and utensils to make fresh corn bread or cake. This includes a one pound bag of corn bread mix from the supermarket, an egg, some buttermilk, and whatever else the recipe calls for. Also, a fresh jar of strawberry jam, some margarine to spread on the hot corn bread, utensils, napkins, a tablecloth, and a big bag with GIGO written on it.

Scripture Lesson: "Religion that God our Father accepts as pure and faultless is this: to look after orphans and widows in their distress and to keep oneself from being polluted by the world" (James 1:27, NIV).

The purpose of this object lesson is to emphasize how sin pollutes a person's life. This works best in a classroom setting where a kitchen oven is available for baking. As you begin mixing the ingredients in a bowl, speak about how our lives should be pure. Point out that the ingredients by themselves are clean and pure before they are mixed together to form a very tasty corn bread.

Once all the ingredients are added and the mixing is done, you have raised the level of anticipation to a high degree. Everyone's mouth is watering for a piece of the freshly baked corn bread. At the height of expectation, announce that there's just one more ingredient to add before the corn bread is baked. Pull out a brown paper sack with GIGO written on the outside in huge letters. The bag contains dirt. GIGO is a computer acronym for "garbage in, garbage out!"

Discussing the meaning of GIGO, emphasize that sin pollutes our lives. Explain *1 Corinthians 3:16, 17: "Surely you know that you are God's temple and that God's Spirit lives in you! . . . For God's temple is holy, and you yourselves are his temple" (TEV).*

133

At this point, focus in on some specific problem that you know of in the group. It may be immorality, filthy language, pornography, or whatever would pollute a person's mind. Children will readily respond to a question that asks if they would bring a trashy magazine to church, or if they would curse or swear or drink beer or smoke a cigarette in the sanctuary. Of course, they're going to be against such things.

At that point, emphasize the words "you are God's temple." Then for dramatic effect, dump the dirt into the pure mix. The kids are repulsed and protest loudly because you have ruined a perfectly good pan of corn bread.

This then gives you the opportunity to discuss the repulsiveness of sin in our lives and underscore the need "to keep oneself from being polluted by the world."

Conclude by pointing the young people to Jesus and explaining that He will gladly clean up their lives if they will let Him. *"If we confess our sins, he is faithful and just to forgive us our sins, and to cleanse us from all unrighteousness" (1 John 1:9).* He will remove the dirt from our lives—something that is impossible for us to do on our own.

Clyde the Crybaby Coconut

Visual Aids: Two coconuts, some craft store eyes and hair, buttons for the nose and the mouth.

Preparation: Take one of the coconuts and carefully drill a hole in the top. Because the shells are easily split, it is best to start with a small drill and then move up to a ½-inch bit. Drain the coconut milk and let the coconut dry several weeks if possible. After drying, place in it a marble, heavy nut, bolt, or something similar that will rattle when you shake it.

Next, glue on the hair, eyes, and other facial features as you wish. The coconut that rattles, Clyde the Crybaby Coconut, is to have a frown; the other, Helen the Happy Coconut, is to have a big smile. The smile and the frown can be made easily by gluing small buttons to the face. The hair hides the drilled hole.

Today I have two guests with me. I'd like to introduce you to Helen the Happy Coconut and Clyde the Crybaby Coconut. Now, on the outside they look very similar, but inside there is a real difference. Helen the Happy Coconut is a pretty little thing with a big smile on her face. She's always happy because she loves Jesus and she knows that He loves her. She is like the text in Proverbs that says: *"A merry heart doeth good like a medicine."* Helen just makes people feel better when she's around.

Next I'd like to introduce you to Clyde the Crybaby Coconut. Clyde is a big baby who is always crying and wanting his way. Maybe you know some kids who are like that. If they don't get their way, they stomp their feet and cry and cry while trying to get their way. Clyde is a lot like the second part of the text, which says: *"A broken spirit drieth up the bones."* Clyde has done a lot of crying, not because he's sad, but because he just wants to get his own way.

As I said earlier, Clyde and Helen look a lot alike on the outside, but inside they are very different. Here's how we can tell the difference—we shake their heads!

At this point let the children take turns shaking the coconuts. The difference is that one rattles and the other swishes the liquid around. [The children always show amazement at the difference in the coconuts and enjoy passing them around and explaining to the others how to make them swish or rattle.]

Now, boys and girls, we know that people are not really like these coconuts. We don't swish or rattle inside when someone shakes us, but we are different inside according to the way we think. We've all met people who are always sad, always complaining, always unhappy. They're just not pleasant people to be around, are they? On the other hand, we know people who are always nice, always happy. These are the people who have merry hearts, and they make everybody around them happy. As the Bible says: *"A merry heart doeth good like a medicine: but a broken spirit drieth the bones" (Prov. 17:22).*

I want to be a happy coconut, don't you?

Walking Carefully
With Your Friends

Visual Aid: Three strands of rope that are partially braided together.

If you're going to go for a long walk with someone, isn't it always more fun to go with a friend? The Bible asks the question: *"Can two walk together, except they be agreed?" (Amos 3:3)*. But I wonder if that question also applies to animals? Are there animals that have to agree on things before they walk together? There certainly are, and a lot of them.

Take, for example, the skinny-legged white bird called the cattle egret. These birds are best friends with cows. As many as seven or eight egrets walk along behind the feet of cattle and eat the crickets, flies, grasshoppers, and other creatures that the bigger animals scare up. These two animals dine at the same table, but eat different foods. They walk along beside each other, but the egrets don't eat grass, and the cows wouldn't think of munching on frogs and toads. From time to time the egrets will even hop on a cow's back and ride. But beware to any bug or fly that lands on the cow's back, because it becomes an instant egret snack. These two animals are definitely agreed as they walk along together.

When I think of the cattle egret and its friend the cow, I also think of friendship between people like you and me. There is a Bible verse that says: *"A rope made of three cords is hard to break" (Eccl. 4:12, TEV)*. Or said another way, when three pieces of rope like this [show the rope] are braided together, they are always stronger than three pieces by themselves.

Like the rope, there are three things that make friendships strong. First, friends need each other. This is the first strand of a great friendship. [Hold up one strand alone.] The cow and the cattle egret can get along without each other, but they do much better when they walk along together.

This is what makes the second strand important [hold up the second strand] they need each other. When the skinny-legged egret is riding on the back of a cow, it is enjoying its meal of flies. When the egret eats the flies, the flies don't get to lay their eggs in the hair of the cow and cause old bossy to have a bad attitude.

This, then, brings us to the third strand that makes up the rope of friendship. Friends appreciate each other. The cow could easily get tired of the cattle egrets hanging around and mash them flat, but that wouldn't made good sense. The egret helps the cow even though it does get under the cow's feet now and then. So the cow appreciates the egret, and the cattle egret appreciates the cow. In this case, two friends are walking together because they are agreed on the three things that make a friendship possible: (1) they need each other, (2) they help each other, and (3) they appreciate each other.

Those are the three cords that make strong Christian friendships. We need each other, we help each other, and we appreciate each other.

The next time you see cattle egrets walking along with the cows, remember those three things that make friendships strong. Needing each other, helping each other, and appreciating each other.

The Devil's Free Cheese

Visual Aid: An old-fashioned spring-type mousetrap.

My neighbor used to keep mice in a jar! Well, it wasn't exactly as bad as it might sound. He would take gallon jars and stuff them full of hay and punch holes in the lid. Then he would catch little gray field mice and keep them in the big jar. He wasn't mean—he fed and watered them every day. After watching how they made their nests and little tunnels through the hay, he would release them back into the field. At worst, the mouse had a short stay in a glass hotel room.

Mice can have a much worse fate if they sneak into people's houses. What a little mouse doesn't know is that there is free cheese in every mousetrap, but there is a terrible price to pay for a bite of cheese!

The same thing goes for us humans. Bad habits start when you nibble on the devil's cheese, and like the little mouse, you soon discover that you must pay a terrible price. Friends may offer you a puff on a cigarette. They always say the same thing: "Go ahead, just one little puff won't kill you." So you give in and try a puff. Your friends were right, it didn't kill you. So a couple of days later you take another puff. When you do that, you're nibbling on the devil's cheese again. Then you try smoking a whole cigarette, and before long you are caught in the trap.

[For dramatic effect, snap the mousetrap here.]

Bad habits start when you nibble on the devil's cheese. Friends may offer you some wine or beer. They always say the same thing: "Go ahead, just one little drink won't kill you." So you give in and take a sip. It tastes terrible! But then a couple of days later you take another sip and then another. You're nibbling on the devil's cheese again. Next you try drinking a whole bottle, and before long you're

139

caught in the trap.

[For dramatic effect, snap the mousetrap here.]

Bad habits start when you nibble on the devil's cheese. Friends may offer you some drugs. They always say the same thing: "Go ahead, just a little won't kill you." So you give in and take some. It tastes terrible! But then a couple of days later you take some more. You're nibbling on the devil's cheese again. Next you try taking even more, and before long you're caught in the trap.

[For dramatic effect, snap the mousetrap here.]

The devil's cheese has one very serious drawback. It produces deadly results. If you eat the devil's free cheese, it will do you in. After all, it is bait in his trap, and what are traps made to do? They're made to hurt you!

[Snap the trap for the last time.]

Please remember that every mousetrap has free cheese. The devil's mousetrap always has free cheese, but just like any other mousetrap, it is designed to trap you! Smart kids, leave the devil's cheese alone!

It's All in the Way You Look at It

Visual Aid: A paper cutout of the bird silhouette included with this story.

How did God create in the animals ways for them to protect themselves? There are three ways: (1) fight back, (2) run, (3) hide.

[Encourage the children to mention the offensive weapons of fangs, claws, hooves, and horns. Next would be speed to escape—birds or deer or anything that can run or fly fast. Next would be stealth or hiding—animals that have camouflage, like a fawn that lies perfectly still until danger has passed, or a stick bug that freezes in place and looks just like a twig so that the bird won't see it.]

This then brings us to our subject of today—baby chicks. How many of you have seen little chicks? We call them peepers because they make a little peeping sound. Did you know that Jesus talked about baby chicks? He said that the people of Jerusalem were like baby chicks: *"How many times I wanted to put my arms around all your people, just as a hen gathers her chicks under her wings, but you would not let me!"* (Matt. 23:37, TEV).

Jesus was talking about how a mother hen protects her little baby chicks. Maybe you have seen a mother hen spread her wings and crowd all her baby chicks underneath to keep them safe. But there is more to the story. God has seen to it that the little chicks were born with a fear of certain shadows. For example, if a chick sees on the ground a shadow of a duck or a goose flying over, it knows not to be afraid. But if the chick sees the shadow of a hawk that is flying overhead, it runs for cover.

Boys and girls, this is a cutout of a bird. What is interesting is how it looks. If I hold it this way, it looks like a duck, but if I turn it around, it looks like a hawk. It's all in the way you look at things. If I were a little chick and saw this shadow on the ground, I would run for cover. If I saw this shadow, I would go on pecking away, looking for something to eat.

God has done many things for us to protect us from danger. He made us much smarter than any birds or animals. God gave us the intelligence to know right from wrong. But we have to learn what is right and what is wrong. That's why we have the teachings of Jesus in the Bible. These teachings help us learn what's right and how to do it.

Jesus was disappointed with the people He called little chicks, because they knew what was right and wouldn't do it. Boys and girls, Jesus has shown us what is right. May we always do it!

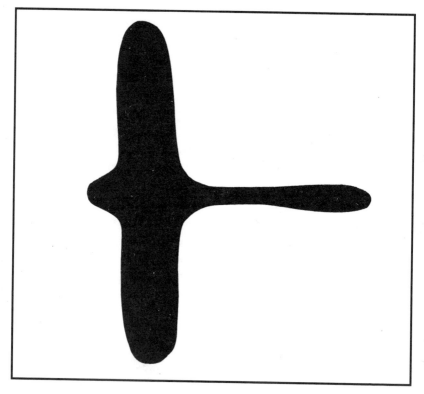

Hilda Hollow Head

This object lesson is to heighten the sensitivity of young people to have more positive attitudes toward other young people.

Visual Aids: 1. A fancy pedestal bowl; the taller, the better. [I use a piece of carnival glass that stands on a pedestal about four inches tall]. 2. A two-liter clear plastic drink bottle with a large hole cut in the back. Put a small "friendship" plant in some dirt inside of the bottle so that it looks like a terrarium. 3. The head of a string mop sawed off from its handle. 4. A large hammer with a big label tied onto it that says "Wally New Student is a four-eyed, freckled-faced, fat fink." 5. Poster board cutouts of eyes, ears, mouth, a bow tie, glasses, and a big nose, all colored in with a felt-tip pen.

[This object lesson works best in a classroom setting and is told as follows.]

How many of you remember your first day in school? Do you remember how it felt to be with all of those strangers and not know anybody? How many of you have ever transferred from one school to another? It's hard to be the new kid in class, isn't it?

This is the story of just such a young person whom I've named Wally New Student. Wally New Student moved and had to attend a new school in a strange town. Wally was a nice boy, even though he had some really big ears. [Tape the ears onto the bottle.]

He read a lot of books and wore big thick glasses, but he was a very nice boy. He was good to his dog and talked to his goldfish every day. [Tape the glasses with the eyes drawn in onto the bottle.]

Wally was always well dressed for a boy who loved computers and science. He was very smart. [Tape on the mouth and bow tie.]

In Wally's new school, the most beautiful girl was named Hilda Hollow Head. [Set out the bowl.] Hilda was a very foxy girl with big beautiful eyes. [Tape eyes onto the front of the dish.] She also had long beautiful hair. [Droop the mop head over the dish.] She was a sight to behold and made every boy's heart go "tur-pocket-a, tur-pocket-a, tur-pock."

On the first day Wally came to school, Hilda immediately didn't like him. She said he looked dumb. She made fun of him behind his back, and all the kids joined in and laughed at Wally simply because Hilda Hollow Head didn't like him.

Poor Wally couldn't have any friends because of Hilda. He was lonely and discouraged. But his mother told him that it was what was inside that really mattered. Wally was like this tender little "friendship plant." Inside he was a beautiful person. [Pick up Wally and turn him so that everyone can see the plant.]

One day after Wally had been coming to school for a week or so, Hilda did a very bad thing. She was jealous because Wally was getting such good grades. So she marched right up to Wally and yelled in his face, "Wally New Student, you're a fat, four-eyed, freckle-faced fink!"

Her words hurt Wally very much. So much that it crushed him. [Take the hammer with the words attached and strike Wally New Student. Flatten the bottle and be sure to break the plant. Invariably the hearers of the story will be upset that you broke the plant. Their affection will be for the tiny plant that you destroyed. That's when you make the point of whether a real person or a plant is more valuable. Remind them of *Proverbs 15:4: "Kind words bring life, but cruel words crush you spirit" (TEV).]*

Larry the Liar

Visual Aid: (See photo.)

Larry the Liar is a large white light bulb with a face drawn on it with felt-tip pens and some hair glued on top for effect. The light bulb is screwed into an old table lamp decorated to look like a schoolboy. Larry's appearance is dependent solely on the storyteller's artistic talent. My Larry the Liar was painted for me by a friend. Going to such extremes is not necessary to make the story a success.

The crucial part of this project is putting an electric dimmer switch on the lamp cord. Although the parts are inexpensive, it does require some electrical knowledge to make it work safely and should be done only by someone who is competent in electrical wiring.

The main point of the visual aid is that the bulb gets brighter every time Larry the Liar lies. Since dimmer switches come with a round knob to control the brightness of incandescent light bulbs, with just a little practice a person can make the bulb brighter and dimmer according to the size of the lie that is being told.

To begin, explain the main point of this lesson—that violating one's conscience by lying can become easier and easier with practice. While the use of Larry the Liar is humorous, the lesson to be learned is serious and easily remembered because of the visual aid.

The Presentation

Boys and girls, have any of you ever told a lie? Many people lie, but that doesn't make it right. That's why I have somebody with me whom I want you to meet. His name is Larry the Liar. Now, Larry started out just like you and me. At first when he told a lie, he could feel his face get hot. Do you know what I mean? That's right. When

you lie, you can feel your ears turn red and your face get hot. Of course, that's a message from your conscience that you have just done something wrong.

Today I'm going to ask Larry some questions and see how he reacts. [Turn the bulb on low so that it glows dimly.]

1. How old are you? [Answer as if talking for Larry and speak the truth. This would also be a good opportunity to use an assistant. The bulb stays at the same brightness because Larry told the truth.]

2. What grade are you in? [Same brightness.]

3. Do you have a sister? [Same brightness.]

4. Are you nice to her? [The bulb glows brighter as he lies.]

5. Did you hit her the other day? [His face tells all as it flashes brighter and brighter.]

[At this point, explain that Larry practices and practices at lying, and he gets better and better. Then start through the questions again.]

1. Do you have a sister?

2. Are you nice to your sister? [Larry glows but only a little.]

3. Do you still hit your sister? [Again Larry is lying, but he is so much better at it that it is hardly noticeable.]

Conclusion

Larry filled his mind with more and more lies. If he kept it up, he would get so good that he would start to believe his own lies. How terrible! The Bible says: *"Fill your minds with those things that are good and that deserve praise: things that are true, noble, right, pure, lovely, and honorable" (Phil. 4:8, TEV).* That's what I want to do, don't you?

The Devil's Doorknobs

Visual Aid: An old white doorknob or a knob painted white.

[This story deals with an abstraction that younger children will not understand. It is a simile that likens a doorknob to evil temptation.]

"Trust in the Lord with all your heart. Never rely on what you think you know. Remember the Lord in everything you do, and he will show you the right way. Never let yourself think that you are wiser than you are; simply obey the Lord and refuse to do wrong" *(Prov. 3:5-7, TEV).*

You can easily fool a chicken into doing something she would not ordinarily do. All you do is place a white doorknob in the chicken's nest, and she will lay an egg beside the doorknob. It's an old farmer's trick to keep the hens laying. The farmer places a fake porcelain egg in the nest—or just an old doorknob would do. A farmer I knew used doorknobs. The doorknob put the idea in the chicken's head that she needed to lay another egg in the nest to keep company with the doorknob. Now, I should tell you that chickens are not very intelligent. Some have been taught to do some simple tricks such as picking up every fifth kernel in a row of kernels. But when a fence was put up with an open end between the chickens and the kernels, she wasn't intelligent enough to find it and walk through. Is it any wonder that hens think a doorknob is an egg?

However, for those of us who are thousands of times more intelligent than chickens, the devil has doorknobs for us. He has a way of getting ideas into our heads that will get us into trouble. The devil's doorknobs look so obvious . . . after we've gotten in hot water.

For instance, would you steal money from a friend? A young person I know saw lying on a table $50 that belonged to another student. He didn't even need the money, but he didn't resist picking up the devil's doorknob. He stole it from his friend and was found out the very next day, and then he confessed. The price he paid for picking up one of the devil's doorknobs was a reputation as a thief and a week's suspension from school.

Another devil's doorknob is tobacco. When baseball players chew it, it's called "spit tobacco." When people smoke it rolled in paper it's called cigarettes. Either way, it has a deadly poison in it called nicotine, which eventually can kill you. The devil lays this doorknob in places where you can find it easily, and then he tempts you to sneak off and try it. It's a deadly trap. Don't pick it up.

The devil has doorknobs lying all over the place, and he is just waiting for you to pick one up. Whether it be money to steal, beer to drink, tobacco to smoke, or drugs to try, remember that the smart thing to do is simply to ask yourself, What would Jesus do? Then you'll always know what to do the next time you see one of the devil's doorknobs.

What to Read

Visual Aids: A telephone book, a cookbook, and a Bible.

Boys and girls, how many of you can read? Do you like to read exciting stories? How many of you like to have stories read to you? Good, because today I'm going to read to you from one of my favorite books. The telephone book! [Open the book and pretend you are going to read. In a mocking way, ask the children, "Do you not want me to read from the telephone book?" Of course, the answer will be no, so ask, "What's wrong with a phone book? Isn't it a useful book? But it has only one purpose, and that is to list phone numbers. That's not very interesting reading, I guess. Would you say it is b-o-r-i-n-g?" Casually take the phone book and toss it on the floor.]

Boys and girls, I have another book with me. Hold up the cookbook for those who can read the title. This will really make for some good reading.

[The children will roll their eyes and immediately begin to react to the reading of part of any recipe that you happen to turn to.]

I guess you're going to say this is not very interesting reading either. Would you say it is also b-o-r-i-n-g? Even though we all like to eat those wonderful things that are made from recipes in cookbooks, just reading from the book can be pretty dull. [Casually take the cookbook and toss it on the floor.]

Boys and girls, I have one more book with me. [Hold up the Bible.] This Book is different. It doesn't have any telephone numbers or recipes for good things to eat, but it does have some very important and exciting things to read in it. It's full of stories about people such as David and Goliath, and Daniel in the lions' den, Mary the handmaid of the Lord, and Esther, the fair and beautiful maid who won a beauty contest and saved her people. Most important of all, the Bible tells us about Jesus and the heaven He has prepared for us—the place where lions, lambs, and you and I will all live in peace together. I want to be there, don't you?

The Bible tells us how to get from here to hereafter. It's not just a telephone book or a cookbook. It's much more than that. It's God's Word—written down for us to read and enjoy. That's what makes our Bibles so special.

Pineapple Pete

Visual aids and preparation needed: A whole pineapple, a can of sweetened pineapple chunks, a nice serving bowl, some toothpicks, and someone to assist who is wearing heavy work gloves. Also needed will be the parts from a Mr. Potato Head or something similar.

[The point of this object lesson is to take something that is ugly on the outside and show that it is beautiful on the inside. Using the plastic eyes, ears, nose, mouth, etc., of the Mr. Potato Head, the presenter turns a pineapple into a person named Pineapple Pete. To make the presentation go without any embarrassing hitches, it is best to assemble the whole unit at home and then disassemble it prior to doing the demonstration before the children. This will leave the holes already punched so that you can reinsert the parts without any trouble when you make the public presentation.]

"When they arrived, Samuel saw Jesse's son Eliab and said to himself, 'This man standing here in the Lord's presence is surely the one he has chosen.' But the Lord said to him, *'Pay no attention to how tall and handsome he is. I have rejected him, because I do not judge as man judges. Man looks at the outward appearance, but I look at the heart'* " (1 Sam. 16:6, 7, TEV).]

Today, young people, I have brought along somebody I would like you to meet. [For dramatic flair, have your assistant, wearing gloves for protection, remove the pineapple from a bag and present it on a plastic plate to catch the drippings.]

This is Pineapple Pete. He's a new kid who just moved into the neighborhood. First thing you'll probably notice is his appearance. It looks like Pete is having a bad hair day!

[Place the little hat on the pineapple while commenting about how messy his hair looks. Using your imagination and gauging the responses of the children, continue by installing the eyes, ears, and mouth. You may want to comment on Pete's complexion, that the outward appearance of Pineapple Pete is not really very good looking.

[However, the point is that we are not to judge people by their outward appearance. Scripture says that man looks at the outward appearance, but God looks at the heart, or what is inside.

[At this time have your assistant bring out the bowl of canned pineapple and pass it under the noses of the children, but don't offer them any to eat. Tell them the pineapple smells good as you move the bowl around. Don't ask the children their opinion, because surely there will be some who do not like pineapple.

[Conclude your presentation by shifting their attention back to Pineapple Pete and emphasizing that Christian young people should not judge people by how they look on the outside. It's what's inside that is important.

[After the church service place the bowl of sweetened pineapple and the toothpicks in the foyer or some appropriate place for everyone to sample.]

Word Power

Visual Aids: Some big flash cards of words.

If someone throws a rock and it hits you, does it hurt? It sure does! But what if someone throws a word at you and hits you right between the eyes, does *that* hurt? Whether a word hurts or not is up to you.

Can words make you sad? It's up to you. They cannot if you don't want them to! You make yourself act sad! Can words make you smile? They cannot if you don't want to smile! You make yourself smile! Think about it. Words don't have hands or arms or even faces or tongues to stick out. When someone says something that's funny, it is you who makes yourself laugh and hold your stomach and jump up and down. Isn't it true that you make yourself act happy or sad? It's up to you to decide how you will react to words.

Words are like little packages that are sent to us. Some come with shiny wrapping and bows, and others come in plain old brown paper sacks. It is our choice to do with the words as we wish. We take them out of their packages, unfold them, and then decide what they mean to us. I'm going to send you some words, and you tell me what they mean to you.

Nice Words and Their Effects

What do you think when someone says these words to you?
I have a puppy.
I think you're cute.
I think you're smart.

Not-So-Nice Words and Their Effects

What do you think when someone says these words to you?

You're stupid.
You look ugly.
You bozo!

Other Words in Packages Full of Meaning

What do you think when someone says these words to you?
My grandma bakes cookies.
My mom loves me.
Jesus is your Friend.

Proverbs 15:4 tells us that *"kind words bring life, but cruel words crush your spirit" (TEV).*

[Additional note: Adjust the word list to fit your individual personality. The intent of the word order is to guide the thinking of the children toward Jesus, eventually taking the word "Jesus" and unwrapping its meaning. Jesus is the ultimate kind word that brings life.]

GREAT STORIES JUST FOR KIDS

Guide's Greatest Stories

These gripping true stories of God's power are packed with amazing endings, incredible adventures, life-changing discoveries, and narrow escapes. Compiled by Randy Fishell, they represent some of the best stories in the history of *Guide* magazine. Paper, 157 pages. US$8.95, Cdn$13.00.

Heart of the Warrior

The kids at Shadow Creek Ranch are about to welcome a whole vanload of guests. Four of the newcomers will stay. One will mysteriously disappear. Young readers will experience heart-stopping twists and turns in this adventure about experiencing and sharing God's unconditional love. Shadow Creek Ranch, book 6. By Charles Mills. Paper, 160 pages. US$5.95, Cdn$8.65.

Nature Quest

James and Priscilla Tucker bring juniors face-to-face with the greatest force they've ever encountered—God's power to create, sustain, save, and make all things new! They'll discover fascinating facts about nature and surprising insights into their Creator. Hardcover, 365 pages. US$9.95, Cdn$14.45.

Available at all ABC Christian bookstores (1-800-765-6955) and other Christian bookstores.

CHARACTER-BUILDING STORIES FOR KIDS

StoryTime With Jack and Carmela

This delightful collection of stories teaches early/middle elementary children valuable lessons about forgiveness, getting along with brothers and sisters, obedience, making friends, and God's love. Parent/user guide inside. Six videos, approximately 30 minutes each. US$9.95, Cdn$14.45 each.

StoryTime Classic Edition 1-3

This premium collection of Uncle Arthur's stories includes all-new color illustrations, plus games and crafts that enhance the character-building lessons. Hardcover three-volume set with slipcase. US$29.95, Cdn$43.45.

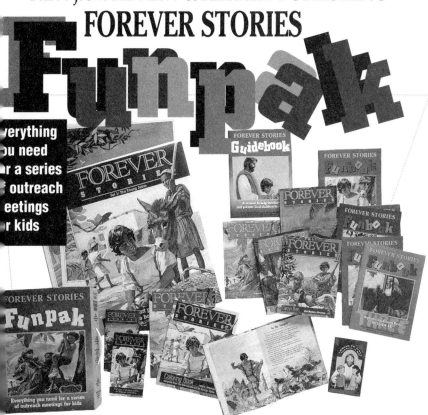